Washington State Gun Rights and Responsibilities

by Dave Workman

FOREWORD

What you are about to read is not a law book, and it is not a substitute for the law. I am not an attorney. I am a certified firearms instructor, with more than 20 years of experience, having taught courses in team scenarios, as a individual, and even on a community college campus.

This book deals with firearms ownership, both the rights and responsibilities, for Washington state residents, and those visiting the state and carrying concealed on Washington concealed pistol licenses or licenses from other states recognized by Washington law. It contains language from existing Washington state statutes that were in effect at the time it was written. This includes the laws that relate to the use of force in self defense, defense of property, and defense of another person.

Read the sections on "Open Carry" in Chapter Four and "No duty to Retreat" in Chapter Five and understand them. Don't be stupid, and don't worry about being a test case on open carry, there already was one, and the defendant lost. See the new Question and Answer section at the end of Chapter Four regarding concealed and open carry.

You will also find advice on safe firearms handling, a section in the rear on kids and guns, and the general "rules of the road" about owning, carrying and using firearms, whether for recreation or personal defense.

Read Chapter Eight on the Do's and Don'ts of concealed carry.

This revised edition includes an updated section with key elements about laws in other states where Washington concealed pistol licenses are recognized, and administrative codes relating to firearms on college campuses.

It is strongly recommended that anyone reading this book who is considering a first-time firearms purchase, or obtaining a Washington state concealed pistol license, seek competent instruction before shooting or carrying a gun.

You will find a listing of good shooting schools at the end of Chapter 5, plus the address of the National Rifle Association, Washington Arms Collectors, Second Amendment Foundation and Citizens Committee for the Right to Keep and Bear Arms, all of which you should join and support.

This book is the result of extensive research and years of experience on the front line of firearms instruction.

It is not intended as a layman's guide on how, and under what circumstances, it is permissible to take a human life, but rather, to avoid becoming a statistic, either as a victim of crime, or of the legal system in Washington state.

A lot of people who fancy themselves firearms and personal defense instructors, and who speak in the jargon of gun magazines and "reality" cop programs on television, have never actually seen or heard a shot fired in anger, never held anyone at gunpoint, never been involved in a potentially lethal confrontation or the arrest of a criminal suspect and have never observed the dead or dying victim of a gunshot wound. I am not one of those people.

DISCLAIMER

The author makes no claim that the explanation of state laws contained herein are how they will be interpreted by the courts. The author further accepts no responsibility for, nor does the author have any control over, the actions of any individual.

It is your responsibility to seek the advice of legal counsel any time a question arises as to a personal situation involving the use of a firearm in defense of yourself or another party.

Dave Workman
North Bend, Washington

Yes, I am 'That' Workman

Many of you have seen advertisements for a "Workman" holster by Mitch Rosen Extraordinary Gunleather. I created the original design for that holster, which I call "The Undershirt," when a shooting buddy asked if I could build a rig over which he could tuck a shirt.

I still build The Undershirt through **D&D Gunleather, P.O. Box 1638, North Bend, WA 98045.** Mitch Rosen, 300 Bedford Street, Manchester, NH 03101-1102, also continues to faithfully produce this holster, and has created a few variations that are superb.

Several other firms have shamelessly copied the design. Get an original

ACKNOWLEDGMENTS

To the authors of Article 1, Section 24 of the Washington State Constitution, which recognizes our individual right to keep and bear arms in defense of ourselves, and the state.

Many thanks to my good friends Bill Churchill, Alan and Julianne Gottlieb and Joe Waldron, and the many firearms retailers and gun range operators who enthusiastically recommend and market this publication. Can't forget my wife, Dacey, who diligently keeps track of the finances at D&D Enterprises and D&D Gunleather.

My gratitude to Massad Ayoob, who has proven himself to be an outstanding friend, as well as an excellent teacher. Likewise, to master holster craftsman Mitch Rosen, and his wife, Nancy. Mitch took a good design and made it great, reminding me along the way that pride is one of those "Seven Deadlies."

Finally, a personal note to some good folks in law enforcement, a few of whom I consider pretty special people, for their continued support. Your friendship has meant a great deal. Some of you owe me one. . .(or two, or three!). I think good thoughts about you. Be careful, go home safe, and always be good to yourselves.

JOIN AND SUPPORT THESE ORGANIZATIONS:

National Rifle Association of America
11250 Waples Mill Road, Fairfax, VA 22030 / (703) 267-1000

Citizens Committee for the Right to Keep and Bear Arms
12500 N.E. Tenth Place, Bellevue, WA 98005 / (425) 454-4911

Washington Arms Collectors
P.O. Box 389, Renton, WA 98057-0389 / (425) 255-8410

Second Amendment Foundation
12500 N.E. Tenth Place, Bellevue, WA 98005 / (425) 454-7012

TABLE OF CONTENTS

Achtung!

The Lautenberg Act'

In September 1996, the U.S. Congress passed a federal statute that prohibits any person, including a police officer, from owning or possessing any firearm or ammunition if he or she has ever been convicted of a domestic violence misdemeanor that included the use, or attempted use, of physical force.

Under the "Lautenberg Act," named for its sponsor, Senator Frank Lautenberg (D-NJ), the prohibition also applies to anyone who has threatened the use of a deadly weapon against a child, spouse, roommate or "significant other."

With such a conviction on your record, if you are found in possession of a firearm or cartridges, the penalty can range to ten years in prison and a fine up to $250,000.

Unlike other statutes, the Bureau of Alcohol, Tobacco and Firearms has announced that this law will be enforced retroactively. That is, it applies to convictions that occurred even before the law was enacted.

This is a federal statute, and it supersedes state law. Until it is successfully challenged in court on constitutional grounds, or repealed by the Congress, it remains in force.

'The Violence Against Women Act'

During the first Clinton Administration, Democrats controlling Congress passed this legislation, which, in layman's terms, makes it a federal violation for anyone who is under a restraining order affecting a domestic relationship to possess a firearm or ammunition. This is commonly known as the Violence Against Women Act.

This is the statute that was at the center of the case of *U.S. v Emerson,* not the Lautenberg Act. The federal law is incorporated in 18 U.S.C. § 922, and the pertinent sections are: (g)(8)(A)(B)(C)(i) and (ii).

The U.S. Fifth Circuit Court of Appeals ruled in October 2001 that this statute, as it relates to the Emerson case, does not violate the individual right to keep and bear arms as affirmed by the Second Amendment to the U.S. Constitution. The U.S. Supreme Court declined to hear the appeal. The Emerson case was remanded back to the District Court in Texas, and the defendant, Dr. Timothy Joe Emerson, was convicted.

Until and unless this federal legislation is overturned by the Supreme Court, or repealed by an act of Congress, it remains in effect.

Chapter One
THE RIGHT TO BEAR ARMS

ARTICLE II: "A well regulated Militia, being necessary to the security of a free State, the right of the people to keep and bear Arms, shall not be infringed." (Second Amendment to the U. S. Constitution.)

ARTICLE I, Sec. 24 "RIGHT TO BEAR ARMS. The right of the individual citizen to bear arms in defense of himself, or the state, shall not be impaired, but nothing in this section shall be construed as authorizing individuals or corporations to organize, maintain or employ an armed body of men." (Washington State Constitution.)

The United States, unlike any other nation on Earth, has stood for more than 225 years as a bastion of individual freedom, and a monument to the principle that individual citizens are free to pursue life, liberty and happiness.

To guarantee that such freedom shall stand, the Founders recognized that certain unalienable rights exist, whether they are put on paper or not. Such rights are of a preexisting nature; not "granted" by the Bill of Rights, but merely recognized by that great document to exist. For example, should the First Amendment be wiped clean from the Bill of Rights, it would not mean the right of free speech, press or religion no longer exists, for one cannot abolish an unalienable right by merely erasing it from a piece of paper. The right exists, for all free men and women to exercise. Upon this, most Constitutional scholars agree.

Into this Bill of Rights was wisely inserted an "insurance policy" against tyranny: the Second Amendment. The U.S. Constitution specifically delineates the people's right to keep and bear arms in general terms to assure that the common militia, which consists of all the people, could never be disarmed. Indeed, Thomas Jefferson wrote: "No free man shall be debarred the use of arms."

Added Patrick Henry: "The great object is that every man be armed. Everyone who is able may have a gun."

Washington State's Constitution carries the principle further, and notes specifically that the individual citizen has the right to bear arms in his own defense, and in defense of the state.

This right is not without certain limits. The right to bear arms is not and was never intended to allow citizens to bear arms carelessly, or with criminal intent. A private citizen may not carry arms in order to menace other individuals or the public at large.

While Virginian Richard Henry Lee, a delegate to the Continental Congress, a signator of the Declaration of Independence and member of the original Senate that passed the Bill of Rights declared: "to preserve liberty, it is essential that the whole body of the people always possess arms, and be taught alike, especially when young, how to use them."

This responsibility has many tenets. A firearm should only be used in a legal manner, not carelessly or recklessly. Firearms are not to be used as instruments of terror. Under Washington state statute, when they are used in defense of self or another innocent party, they must be used only "*.. when there is a reasonable ground to apprehend a design on the part of the person slain to commit a felony or to some great personal injury to the slayer or to any such person, and there is imminent danger of such design being accomplished; or ...In the actual resistance of an attempt to commit a felony upon the slayer, in his presence or upon or in a dwelling or other place of abode, in which he is .*"

While there has been, and will continue to be, much debate on the meaning of the Second Amendment, clearly there can be no mistaking that the Washington State Constitution considers the right to bear arms to be an individual right.

> ***"There can be no mistaking that the Washington State Constitution considers the right to bear arms to be an individual right."***

The U.S. Fifth Circuit Court of Appeals in New Orleans ruled in the case of *U.S. v Emerson* that the Second Amendment protects an individual right to keep and bear arms, "regardless of whether the particular individual is then actually a member of the militia."

In its 2-1 ruling on the meaning of the Second Amendment, written by Judge William Garwood, the appeals court acknowledged that this position runs contrary to rulings by other appellate courts relating to the Second Amendment. Other decisions have suggested that it protects only a "collective right" that allows states to arm militias. Scholarly research by academics, and now the court, suggests that the earlier rulings have been in error, and that the Second Amendment protects an individual citizen's right to keep and bear arms, subject to "reasonable regulation."

Of particular importance to the reader: The U.S. Supreme Court has never ruled that the Second Amendment is merely a "collective right" as some gun control advocates erroneously insist.

However, Fifth Circuit Court reversed a lower court ruling that defendant Timothy Joe Emerson's Second Amendment right to keep and bear arms was violated by the 1994 Violence Against Women Act (VAWA). Emerson, involved in a divorce, had been served with a restraining order. Under VAWA (see Appendix), persons subject to such restraining orders may not purchase or possess firearms. Emerson was ultimately convicted.

It must be noted that the Fifth Circuit's individual rights interpretation may only be accepted as applicable to jurisdictions within the Fifth Circuit, which includes Texas, Louisiana and Mississippi. Washington state is within the Ninth Circuit, and that appellate court is located in San Francisco, Ca. The Ninth Circuit does not share the Fifth Circuit's opinion on the meaning of the Second Amendment.

A Report of the Subcommittee on the Constitution of the Committee on the Judiciary, United States Senate, Ninety-Seventh Congress, issued in February 1982, insisted then that the Second Amendment protects an individual right. It was the committee's opinion 20 years ago that the Second Amendment is not merely a collective right, as many gun control proponents would continue having us believe. It now appears the courts are beginning to catch up with constitutional scholars and congressional researchers.

Wrote U.S. Senator Orrin G. Hatch (R-Utah), chairman of the subcommittee:

"In my studies as an attorney and as a United States Senator, I have constantly been amazed by the indifference or even hostility shown the Second Amendment by courts, legislatures, and commentators."

IN WASHINGTON STATE

In 1985, the Washington Legislature took a bold step and passed into law a peremptory act which placed the authority for firearms regulation solely in the hands of the state. By so doing, the Legislature prohibited cities and counties from passing any gun laws that conflicted with, or were more stringent than, those passed by the Legislature. Thus, firearms laws apply statewide. What is legal in King County is also legal in Spokane County.

Since 1997, under the language of RCW 9.41.050, it has been legal statewide to carry rifles and shotguns in the window racks of your vehicle. However, this "open carry" statute does not specifically authorize someone to openly carry a handgun in public. See Chapters 3 and 4.

Fees charged by the state and issuing agencies for concealed pistol license application and renewal are included in the fee schedule found in RCW 9.41.070 (Paragraph 5): *"thirty-six dollars plus additional charges imposed by the Federal Bureau of Investigation that are passed on to the applicant."* At this writing, that amount was $24, which brings the cost of an original application to $60 (bearing in mind that this language allows the state to hike that fee if the FBI increases its charge for running background checks). The cost of renewal remains at $32 and the license is good for a period of five years. To replace a lost or stolen CPL costs $10.

Until such time as restrictive gun laws are changed or repealed by the Legislature, or thrown out by the courts, they remain on the books, and law enforcement agencies will continue to enforce them.

When the Supreme Court overturned the Brady Law in June 1997, it left intact a five day waiting period that expired when the National Instant Check

System (NICS) became operational. The ruling did not alter state law, which provides for a background check, and a five-day (five business days) wait on handgun purchases for citizens who do not have a valid, current concealed pistol license. Essentially, nothing changed here.

In November 1998, the federal instant-check system went on line, and the applicable sections of the Brady Law expired. Now, all firearm purchases are subject to the Instant Check, including all long guns and handguns. But readers should take note of the following:

• Non-CPL holders must go through NICS and the state's five-day wait for delivery of handgun, but not long guns. This wait can extend to seven or eight days, as weekends and holidays do not count.

• Long gun purchases are all subject to the Insta-Check.

• Purchasers having CPL's require a NICS check on any firearm purchase, but the state-imposed five business day waiting period for the delivery of a handgun is waived. That is, you may legally take delivery of a handgun on the day of purchase if you have a current, valid CPL and you pass the NICS check.

The Insta-Check is not "instant." It may take anywhere from several minutes to hours, and up to three days, so be patient.

It must be noted that Washington state laws do not apply to other states. State firearms laws vary considerably.

For example, California currently mandates a 10-day waiting period on the purchase of all firearms, not just handguns. Many Californians learned the harsh reality of waiting periods during the infamous "Rodney King Riot" in Los Angeles in 1992, when the wait was a horrendous 15 days. With the city in chaos, the police unable or unwilling to respond to rioting, the National Guard and the U.S. Marines not yet deployed to bring order, citizens were left to fend for themselves. The first order of business was defense, yet when they rushed to gun stores, they were confronted with the ugly truth of waiting periods: They only serve to restrict the rights, and endanger the safety, of honest citizens. The gangs, the looters, the lawbreakers were subject to no such inconvenience.

A study funded by the Justice Department, and conducted by Profs. James D. Wright and Peter H. Rossi, determined, among other things, that, "...(S)uch evidence as exists on crime deterrence by private weaponry does not support the argument that guns are useless in deterring crime. The evidence does make it quite plain that most crime occurs in circumstances where the victim would have little or no chance to use a gun, even if one were possessed. On the other hand, in the relatively few cases in which there is opportunity to defend oneself with a gun, the evidence suggests that one is somewhat less likely to be successfully victimized if one is armed, than if not." Their findings were published in a book entitled *Under The Gun* in 1983 with Kathleen Daly.

A more recent study, published in 1996 by Prof. John Lott, Jr. and David B. Mustard, University of Chicago, concluded: "allowing citizens to carry concealed weapons deters violent crimes, and it appears to produce no increase in accidental deaths." Their research concluded that areas with high percentages of gun ownership and licensed concealed carry actually have experienced a decline in violent crime, while other areas with restrictive gun laws have seen no similar decline.

As this book went to press, 38 states have "shall issue" or "right-to-carry" laws on the books. Only four states at this writing did not have some form of licensed concealed carry: Illinois, Kansas, Nebraska and Wisconsin.

Whether you choose to exercise your right to keep and bear arms for self protection is a personal matter. Rest assured, a growing number of constitutional scholars, including Harvard's Laurence Tribe, have concluded — against their personal philosophy — that this right is an individual one. They even begrudgingly admit that assertions by anti-gunners — that the Second Amendment only refers to a militia (which they translate to mean today's National Guard) — are essentially bogus. Many cite the writings of the Founders as support for their position.

As observed by Richard Henry Lee, one of the Founders, "A militia, when properly formed, are in fact the people themselves... and include all men capable of bearing arms."

Justice Clarence Thomas, voting with the Majority in overturning Brady, noted: "The Second Amendment. . .appears to contain an express limitation on the government's authority. . .This Court has not had recent occasion to consider the nature of the substantive right safeguarded by the Second Amendment. If, however, the Second Amendment is read to confer a personal right to 'keep and bear arms,' a colorable argument exists that the Federal Government's regulatory scheme, at least as it pertains to the purely intrastate sale or possession of firearms, runs afoul of that Amendment's protections. . .Perhaps, at some future date, this Court will have the opportunity to determine whether Justice Story was correct when he wrote that the right to bear arms 'has justly been considered, as the palladium of the liberties of a republic'."

The information contained in this book is designed to help you not simply reach the decision, but offer some guidance on your rights, responsibilities and legal limitations.

Chapter Two
GUN SAFETY

Despite media hysteria to the contrary, gun accidents are far down the list of causes of death in the United States, and even in Washington state. However, this is no excuse for a gun owner to become lax or careless about firearm safety. Accidents happen because someone does something stupid and handles a firearm negligently.

Beginning in October 2001, the office of the Lieutenant Governor, in cooperation with the State Patrol, other law enforcement agencies, and community groups began giving away free cable gun locks. It is part of a program sponsored by the National Shooting Sports Foundation, with the support of a grant from the Justice Department. The program is called Project HomeSafe.

You are more likely to die in a fall, auto accident or from natural causes than a gunshot wound.

Thanks to successful firearms safety training courses offered by the National Rifle Association through local gun clubs and gun shops, and to the efforts of volunteer Hunter Education instructors across the country, the actual per capita rate of firearms accidents has been steadily declining over the past several decades.

At the core of these programs are the "golden rules" of firearms safety:

• Always keep a firearm pointed in a safe direction. Never point a firearm at anything you do not intend to shoot. (Variation: Never point a firearm at anything you are not willing to destroy.)

• Treat every firearm as if it were loaded until you have personally checked it.

• Keep your finger off the trigger until ready to shoot.

Other rules of firearms safety that should also be taken to heart.

• Be sure of your target and what is beyond it before pressing the trigger. (Note: In hunter education classes, they teach you to think about your "backstop." In shooting investigations involving police officers, one of the questions typically asked by investigating officers is "What was your backstop?")

• Never load a gun until you are ready to use it, and unload it when you are finished using it.

• Use only ammunition intended for your firearm. Modern firearms have the caliber marked on the barrel, and this must match the caliber designated on the cartridge box, and on the cartridge rim. This is called the head stamp.

• Wear adequate eye and ear protection while shooting.

• Keep the barrel and action clear of obstructions.

• NEVER take drugs or drink alcohol before or while shooting or hunting.

Be aware that additional safety precautions may need to be taken depending upon individual circumstances.

This applies particularly to hunting, for which all first-time hunters born after January 1, 1972 must successfully complete the state's hunter education course before they purchase a hunting license.

Only a complete fool picks up a firearm and carries it around without checking to see if it is loaded. Only someone who is criminally inept points a firearm carelessly at another person and pulls the trigger.

By the same token, the person who carries a firearm for personal protection, or for any other reason, should always know its condition.

The absolute rock bottom line of firearms safety is that there is no such thing as a gun accident that cannot be prevented. The terminology of gun mishaps is even changing for that reason. What has long been called an "accidental discharge," meaning that a firearm goes off unintentionally, is now called a "negligent discharge."

If you don't know how a particular gun operates, don't touch it until you have received instructions from a competent, qualified instructor.

The NRA has a network of qualified instructors, and there are other firearms professionals who offer advanced levels of training. Be advised that there are also a legion of people who only think they are competent instructors. Avoid these people at all costs. Typically, local gun clubs or gun shops can refer you to a competent instructor.

Firearms safety is part education and part common sense. The very last place anyone should look for an example of safe gun handling is the television, and particularly cop shows. They feature horrible violations of accepted gun safety rules.

Many television westerns are nearly as bad.

Worse than all of these are the typical action movies with heroes firing pistols in both hands, often while diving for cover, and frequently held sideways. This may look okay on the screen, but gun professionals cringe when they see anyone trying to imitate that hogwash on the firing range.

You want gun safety advice that is good? Find a competent instructor, check out a video entitled "Handgun Safety," that was produced by the National Rifle Association, and pay attention to both.

You want to remain competent with a firearm? Practice. And practice some more.

Chapter Three
WHAT IS LEGAL

In declaring the Brady Law's required federal background check by local police departments unconstitutional, the U.S. Supreme Court did not reverse Washington State's five-day waiting period or background check.

It remains legal for any adult age 21 or over who has not been convicted of a serious felony or certain serious misdemeanors (including domestic violence) to purchase a handgun, under RCW 9.41.070 and RCW 9.41.090, and especially under the provisions of Title 18 U.S.C. § 922 (Gun Control Act of 1968).

The five-day waiting period (five business days, not calendar days) for handgun purchases applies to everyone, including police officers, with some exceptions, outlined on Page 4. The Insta-Check requirement applies to all firearm purchases, including long guns.

It is unlawful for any person under 18 years of age to have a firearm in his or her possession unless accompanied by a parent, guardian or other adult, or a certified safety instructor, under the provisions of RCW 9.41.042.

However, it is legal under RCW 9.41.240 for a person between the ages of 18 and 21 to possess a pistol, provided it is in that person's place of abode, or in the person's fixed place of business, or on real property under his or her control. RCW 9.41.050 allows transport under certain conditions.

And it should also be noted that under the provisions of Title 18 U.S.C. § 922 and Washington law, it is allowed by GCA '68 for a person over age 18 to purchase a rifle or shotgun.

It is also unlawful in Washington, under RCW 77.15.460 for anyone to carry a loaded rifle or shotgun in any motor vehicle, or a loaded handgun for anyone not licensed to carry a concealed firearm under RCW 9.41.070. The prohibition against carrying long guns loaded in vehicles is also part of the state game code.

For more complete details on carrying a concealed firearm, see Chapter Four and the Appendix, where the texts of RCW 9.41.070 and RCW 9.41.300 are found. More complete information on long guns is in Chapter Six.

Washington state law prohibits ownership of fully automatic machine guns and submachine guns by private citizens. A machine gun is any firearm that, with a single squeeze of the trigger, fires multiple shots. A semi-automatic firearm, though it cycles the action and rechambers a cartridge or shotshell without manual assistance, requires a separate trigger squeeze for each shot.

The National Firearms Act of 1934, passed as an anti-criminal law and tax law, outlawed ownership of full-auto firearms for anyone not licensed by the Treasury Department.

Possession of semi-automatic rifles, shotguns and handguns with magazine capacities in excess of ten cartridges is legal.

Essentially, it is legal to own any bolt-action, lever-action, slide-action, double- and single-barrel sporting shotgun or rifle. It is also legal to own any single-action or double-action revolver or semi-automatic pistol, rifle or shotgun that meets the magazine and other cosmetic requirements as set down in federal statute.

Legal, that is, provided you are not a convicted felon, have never been adjudicated mentally incompetent or confined to a mental institution, are not under criminal indictment, on parole or probation. Also, anyone dishonorably discharged from the military is ineligible to own a firearm. And, you may not rush out and purchase a firearm, especially a handgun, if you are free on bond or personal recognizance pending criminal trial, appeal or sentencing for a crime, or under a court order relating to domestic violence or harassment.

It is legal to carry a concealed firearm without a concealed carry license in your place of business or residence. You may carry a rifle or shotgun in the field on state or federal lands where local regulations allow. It is not legal to carry a loaded rifle or shotgun in national, state, county or city parks, on federal military reservations, Indian reservations or the Hanford Nuclear Reservation, with the exception being individuals who obtain special permits to hunt on military or Indian reservations during the hunting seasons.

You may have a loaded rifle or shotgun in your home or business. You may have a loaded rifle, shotgun or handgun outdoors on public or (with permission from the landowner) private land for lawful purposes, virtually any time of the year. (It is prudent to have a valid hunting license if you carry a firearm in the forest or field anytime during an established hunting season!) Again, for more details on long guns, see Chapter Six.

To transport a firearm, it is legal to travel inside Washington with a rifle, shotgun or handgun, provided they are unloaded, with the exception being that those with valid CPLs may have a loaded handgun in the vehicle. Under current state law, unloaded long guns may be carried openly in window racks.

Under current language, persons carrying loaded, concealed handguns must have a valid CPL in his or her possession, and display it upon demand to any police officer or other person when required to do so.

If traveling across state lines, it is legal to transport a firearm in a closed case, in an area not immediately accessible from the passenger compartment. If you are driving a station wagon or SUV, put the gun, unloaded, in a case. When traveling by air, it is absolutely forbidden by federal law to carry a firearm loaded or unloaded, or even a toy gun, on board an aircraft. All firearms must be declared at the baggage counter, and shipped in the baggage compartment unloaded. The case in which the firearm is carried must be locked, and all ammunition must be carried in its original factory container, or in another hard container that is secure.

Airline travel with firearms is discussed in greater detail in Chapter Seven.

TRANSIT VEHICLES, STATE FERRIES

Washington State has the most extensive ferry system in the the country, and state ferries are considered part of the state highway system. As such, it is legal to transport firearms in your vehicles aboard a state ferry. Persons licensed to carry concealed handguns may do so, and that applies to citizens from other states whose licenses to carry are recognized by Washington State.

During periods of high terror alert, vehicles boarding state ferries may be randomly searched for firearms and explosives. If you are legally in possession of firearms, there should be no reason for authorities to prohibit your passage on a state ferry, provided the ferry is not enroute to a Canadian port. You may not transport a firearm into Canada without prior authorization, and transporting handguns into Canada for specific purposes (competition) is strictly regulated. Under most circumstances, your handgun will not be allowed.

It is legal under Washington RCW 9.41.025 (1)(e) to carry a firearm on board a municipal transit bus, provided that this is done so "in a way that is not otherwise prohibited by law." This means you are allowed to carry an unloaded rifle, handgun or shotgun in a case, and if your are licensed to carry under RCW 9.41.070, it is legal to carry concealed on a bus.

SHIPPING FIREARMS

To ship firearms from one state to another, you should ship them via UPS or another common carrier, though decisions by those private firms not to ship, or how to ship, have created headaches for gun owners. The most common example is shipping a firearm back to the factory for repairs, or to a gun shop for modifications. It is not necessary to have a federally licensed gun shop handle the shipping. It may be shipped via Federal Express or UPS, provided those carriers will take your firearm shipment. The firearm must be unloaded.

If shipping from one individual to another, however, that must be done through a federally licensed firearms dealer, someone who possesses a federal firearms license. For example, if you ship a rifle to your brother in another state, you must have it shipped by a local FFL-holder to another FFL- holder in your brother's home state.

If you are traveling, it is legal to ship a firearm to yourself in care of another address, so long as nobody else opens the package.

Under current federal law, it is legal to purchase ammunition and have it shipped to your home.

It must be noted that firearms laws can change and it is incumbent upon the individual to make himself or herself aware of and familiar with such changes.

Also, check ahead with authorities in states where you may be traveling, and ask about any local laws, just to be safe.

Chapter Four
CONCEALED CARRY

Approximately 240,000 Washington residents are legally licensed to carry a concealed handgun, making the Evergreen State among the highest per capita in the nation with lawfully armed private citizens.

Washington's concealed carry statute is RCW 9.41.070. Under this statute, a license to carry a concealed handgun shall be issued to any applicant for the purpose of protection or while engaged in business, sport or while traveling. It was the first of what many consider today's progressive concealed carry laws.

"Shall issue" means that law enforcement officials may not use their frequently arbitrary discretion when issuing CPLs. In other states, where the issuance of CPLs is entirely up to the discretion of local officials, it is typical that only the influential elite are licensed, while the general law abiding public must either go unarmed, or carry concealed firearms illegally. This is why citizens in so many other states have demanded the "shall issue" standard, and lawmakers have followed their wishes, though not without some resistance.

Washington legislators, mindful of this situation, determined that it would not happen here. Efforts have been mounted, specifically by anti-gun public officials in larger metropolitan areas, to change this mandate. At this writing, they have remained unsuccessful.

Under RCW 9.41.070, a CPL must be issued within 30 days of application with the following exceptions: If the applicant does not have a valid permanent Washington driver's license or Washington state identification card or has not been a resident of the state for the previous consecutive 90 days, the issuing authority shall have up to 60 days after the date of application to issue the license.

Applicants may be refused a CPL for several reasons. These include:

• Being ineligible to possess a firearm under the provisions of RCW 9.41.040;

• Is free on bond or personal recognizance pending trial, appeal, or sentencing for a serious offense;

• Is under 21 years of age;

• Is subject to a court order or injunction regarding firearms (i.e., a domestic violence case or restraining order);

• Has an outstanding warrant for his or her arrest from any court of competent jurisdiction for a felony;

• Has been ordered to forfeit a firearm under RCW 9.41.098(1) (d) within one year before filing an application;

• Has been convicted of crimes against children or other persons.

So, what about carrying concealed? Once licensed, it is incumbent upon the individual to be responsible and to truly conceal that sidearm. In the words of one lethal force expert: "Don't be a putz."

Some people get the urge to "flash" their gun, or they wear a short vest or jacket fully with the intention of allowing the bottom end of their holster to project out from below the garment. This is not simply stupid, it might also be considered "menacing" with a firearm, should some observer call the police. It's a fast way to lose your concealed carry license, and rightfully so.

The legally armed citizen must take great pains to conceal his/her firearm. After all, it is nobody's business whether you are carrying; ideally they never know. If you have the urge to flash the gun, leave it at home until your testosterone level drops. Stroking your own ego can end up with your public humiliation, at the very least.

We will discuss this in greater detail in Chapter 8.

You may not carry in any national park, military post or other federal facility, including a federal courthouse, Post Office or any other federally owned or leased building where federal employees regularly work, including U.S. Forest Service ranger stations. This prohibition applies across the United States, and not just in Washington state.

Persons licensed under RCW 9.41.070 may carry concealed handguns in city, county and state parks, despite the frequent presence of signs in many of these park facilities declaring that firearms are not permitted. That is a general prohibition, but RCW 9.41.290 preempts cities, towns and counties from enacting ordinances more stringent or in conflict with, state statute. Persons licensed under RCW 9.41.070 are generally exempted under the language of and RCW 9.41.300, with the one major exception being outdoor music festivals. Concealed carry, even licensed, is prohibited at outdoor music festivals. This especially applies to the Columbia Gorge concerts, which are held on private property. (See RCW 70.108.150 in the Appendix.)

Many, if not most, hospitals are posted against concealed carry. If they are private hospitals, the administrators have the right to prohibit firearms on the premises. Same goes with any other private business. You can take your business elsewhere.

Concealed carry is also prohibited inside the restricted access areas of a jail, law enforcement facility or mental institution. Concealed firearms are also specifically prohibited in courtrooms or in any area of a building used in connection with court proceedings (jury rooms, judges chambers, offices and areas used to conduct business, waiting areas, etc.) See text of RCW 9.41.300 in the Appendix.

In 1995, following a highly publicized shooting in the King County Courthouse in Seattle, the presiding Superior Court judge ordered screening and metal detectors be installed at the entrances of all courthouses in that county.

If you carry concealed, and must go to court, state law requires that the local authorities provide either a stationary locked box sufficient in size for storing pistols (with a key to be provided to the weapon owner), or designate an official to receive weapons for safekeeping during the owner's visit to restricted areas of the building.

Translation: Check your gun, pardner.

Once you retrieve your firearm, you must leave the facility immediately.

Another prohibited place for concealed carry is inside a tavern or cocktail lounge; *"That portion of an establishment classified by the state liquor control board as off-limits to persons under 21 years of age."*

The authorities, or proprietor of said establishment, must post signs designating where weapons are prohibited.

Take special note: Under the provisions of RCW 9.41.098 (1)(e), *"The superior courts and the courts of limited jurisdiction of the state may order forfeiture of a firearm which is proven to be:*

In the possession of a person who is in any place in which a concealed pistol license is required, and who is under the influence of any drug or under the influence of intoxicating liquor, as defined in chapter 46.61 RCW."

Translation: If you are arrested for driving under the influence (drunk driving) and convicted, your firearm will be confiscated. Indeed, if you're armed when arrested, you will lose the gun on the spot, and the court, upon conviction, can order the firearm forfeited permanently.

Also, under provisions of RCW 9.41.040, three convictions for driving a motor vehicle or operating a vessel while under the influence of intoxicating liquor or any drug will cost you your right to possess any firearm.

You may not carry concealed in any public or private elementary or secondary school, or on the grounds, or areas of any facilities while being used exclusively by public or private schools, except as permitted under the guidelines of RCW 9.41.280 (see below).

For example, this restriction applies to public stadiums on the nights of the high school state playoffs.

However, it does not apply to those facilities in the event there is a school group visiting during a professional baseball or football game, or other professional event. There is some dispute whether a prohibition on concealed carry at Seattle's Safeco Field and at Qwest Field is enforceable, since those facilities were partly paid for with public tax money. That question may be answered legally at a later date, but take the author's advice and avoid being a test case.

By the same token, if you do carry in such a facility, **do not** go into the "Tap Room." In fact, don't drink at all!

A careful check of the Washington Administrative Code shows that every state university, community college campus and even vocational/technical schools has enacted some type of prohibition against carrying firearms. Wording of the exact regulation may vary from school to school.

For example, at several institutions, the regulation prohibits: *"Possession or use of firearms, explosives, dangerous chemicals or other dangerous weapons or instrumentalities on the college campus, except for authorized college purposes or for law enforcement officers, unless written approval has been obtained from the dean of student services or any other person designated by the president."* (WAC 132H-120-200 (3)(k))

Several community colleges share this regulation: *"No person or group may use or enter onto college facilities having in their possession firearms, even if licensed to do so, except commissioned police officers as prescribed by law."* (WAC 132U-140-040, Section 9)

At the University of Washington, under WAC 478-124-020 (2)(e) *"Possession or use of firearms, explosives, dangerous chemicals or other dangerous weapons or instrumentalities on the university campus, except for authorized university purposes, unless prior written approval has been obtained from the vice president for student affairs, or any other person designated by the president of the university"* is prohibited.

(This WAC restriction also applies to licensed private citizens visiting Harborview Medical Center in Seattle, which is administered by the University of Washington.)

Yet at Central Washington University, WAC 106-124-700 provides the following restrictions on firearms, explosives and dangerous chemicals:

No person shall have in his possession any gun, pistol, firearm, explosive, dangerous chemicals, or other dangerous weapons or instruments on university-owned or university-leased property except as follows:

(1) Authorized law enforcement officers shall be permitted to carry arms while on duty and engaged in their regular duties;

(2) Activities requiring use of the prohibited items may be conducted upon approval of the president or his designee;

(3) Persons with firearms in their possession shall be permitted to travel enroute to or from the university-provided firearm storage facilities only. Violators of this WAC shall be subject to appropriate disciplinary or legal action.

As you can see, rules change a bit from campus to campus, but the bottom line is that your legally licensed concealed handgun is not welcome. While the WAC regulations appear to fly in the face of state pre-emption, that fact may be immaterial in a court. Don't try to be a test case.

Under RCW 9.41.280, it is permitted to carry firearms on school property if you are involved in a convention, showing, demonstration, lecture or firearms safety course authorized by school authorities. It is also allowable, under Subsection (3)(e) of this statute for the licensed private citizen to possess a sidearm "while picking up or dropping off a student."

However, you can't linger. There is some disagreement about what is permitted under this Subsection, whether it actually allows concealed carry inside a school building.

As mentioned before, you may not carry a concealed firearm through or beyond the security checkpoints of an airport. Should you try, you will be detained and quite probably arrested, and your firearm will be confiscated. You may lose your CPL, too.

IN YOUR VEHICLE

Under the provisions of RCW 9.41.050 (2). *"A person shall not carry or place a loaded pistol in any vehicle unless the person has a license to carry a concealed pistol and: (a) The pistol is on the licensee's person, (b) the licensee is within the vehicle at all times that the pistol is there, or (c) the licensee is away from the vehicle and the pistol is locked within the vehicle and concealed from view from outside the vehicle."*

Does this allow a licensed person to carry a loaded gun in his/her vehicle, say under the seat, in the console or glove compartment? YES. Is it smart? NO.

In a letter dated March 13, 1987 to then-Sen. Kent Pullen, Senior Assistant Attorney General Richard A. Heath wrote, in response to an inquiry about carry in a vehicle under RCW 9.41.050, "...the plain language of the statute, internal consistency and legislative intent all require an affirmative answer to your question. RCW 9.41.050 permits a person who possesses a valid concealed weapon permit, and who is within a vehicle, to legally posses a loaded pistol within the vehicle which is not on his or her person."

Let's be practical, and prudent for a moment. As a firearms instructor, the author's advice is to carry the firearm on your person, regardless what the law allows according to Heath's interpretation. There are several reasons.

If you have passengers, particularly children, would you want them to discover a loaded firearm and begin waving it around in a car you are driving, with the potential for accidental discharge and tragedy?

If you are the victim of a car jacking, and are ordered from the car, or taken hostage, would you want yourself suddenly separated from your defensive firearm, even by the distance of a few feet?

If you are in an auto crash, would you want that firearm flying around the inside of your vehicle at a centrifugal force speed that might approach 50 to 100 m.p.h.?

The answer to all three questions is a definite **NO**.

What about traffic stops? If you are pulled over by a police officer for any reason, and you are carrying your firearm, keep your hands in clear view on the steering wheel as the officer approaches.

Washington state statute has no provision requiring that an armed citizen immediately present his or her concealed pistol license to a police officer during a traffic stop. In other states, for example Michigan, where a Washington CPL is honored, you are required to display your CPL immediately, thus alerting the officer that you are armed. In Ohio and Utah, for example, you must immediately advise a peace officer that you are armed and have a license to carry.

Here in Washington, the officer will almost certainly ask to see your driver's license, and may even ask you to step from the vehicle. At that point, it is prudent to advise the officer in language something like this: "Officer, I'm licensed to carry a concealed weapon, and I am wearing it now. What would you like me to do?"

There are a couple of fundamentally sound reasons for this approach. First and foremost, police officers don't like surprises, like seeing a firearm on someone's hip as he/she is reaching for a wallet. You could end up staring at the business end of his or her sidearm. Secondly, volunteering the information and "putting the ball in his/her court" tends to establish your good intentions as an honest citizen. Third, in the event you are stopped by a two-man car, one officer will approach the driver's side door, and remain just slightly to the rear, while the other officer will position himself or herself on the passenger side, in a position behind you, where he/she can observe your movements.

> ***"Starting an argument with a police officer when you are armed is monumentally stupid. Invariably, you are going to lose."***

Now, should you have a firearm stuffed in the glove compartment, lying on top of the registration, how's that going to look to an officer if you suddenly move toward a handgun?

Spare yourself the grief.

Wear the firearm on your person, declare it if and when you are asked to step out of the vehicle, and keep a cool head. Nobody enjoys being pulled over by the police, but starting an argument with a police officer (in police parlance this is called "flunking the attitude test"), especially when you are armed, is monumentally stupid. Invariably, you are going to lose. Your attitude, and actions, reflect on every legally licensed armed citizen in the state. Besides, a good attitude and non-confrontational demeanor could draw nothing more than a stern warning from an officer who does have considerable discretion at this point.

It might be also prudent to have your wallet out and ready on the dash board near the wheel when the officer approaches, and at night, turn on the dome light to illuminate the interior of your vehicle. Rest assured, he/she is watching your movements from the moment your vehicles come to a stop. Trying to stash a gun under the seat sends a very wrong signal; you are either trying to hide something, or are reaching for something. An officer who is determined to end his/her shift still alive is going to be put on alert, and you really don't want a traffic stop to escalate into something more than that.

Women who carry their licensed handgun in a purse should not be rummaging around in that bag for a driver's license. It's a very bad idea to carry a gun in your purse, because purses can be snatched, even from your car seat when stopped at a traffic signal.

Women should adopt an alternate means of carry, whether in a fanny pack (many models are available that are designed specifically for concealed carry), or in one of the many superb nylon or leather holsters now available.

A word of caution here: An officer may ask to take possession of your handgun "for *officer* safety." You are under no legal obligation to surrender your pistol to that officer. This is a matter of personal discretion, and if you do turn over your pistol, expect to get it back unloaded.

Here's what one veteran cop explained to me about this: "To my knowledge there is no statutory requirement for a licensed private citizen to hand over his pistol to a police officer during a routine traffic stop. However, court precedent and police officer training allows the officer to take necessary and reasonable steps to assure his own safety and the safety of others. The officer's determination for doing so would be based on the...circumstances and the officer's subjective view of the situation."

There is one instance in which you might be far better off, strictly in the interest of public safety, to tell the officer politely that your pistol is plenty safe right where it is. This is in the event you are carrying a cocked, and locked, single-action Model 1911-type pistol.

Contrary to what many politicians and reporters might believe, many cops are not firearms experts. A cocked, locked .45-caliber pistol in the hands of an individual who is used to handling double-action semi-auto pistols with "hammer-drop" safeties could be a disaster.

There are exemptions to the requirement of possessing a concealed carry license, found in RCW 9.41.060. They primarily apply to law enforcement officers and members of the armed forces while on duty.

However, Paragraph (8) of that section specifically exempts *"Any person engaging in a lawful outdoor recreational activity such as hunting, fishing, camping, hiking, or horseback riding,"* and Paragraph (9) exempts *"Any person while carrying a pistol unloaded and in a closed opaque case or secure wrapper."*

There are also exemptions in the same chapter for *"regularly enrolled members of clubs organized for the purpose of modern and antique firearm collecting..."*

You may also carry concealed without a license in your home or fixed place of business.

Original application requires a lengthy background check. As noted previously in this chapter, for individuals who have been a Washington state resident for less than 90 days, this process can take up to 60 days. For long-time residents, the process may take up to 30 days.

However, with the exceptions explained earlier in this chapter, Washington state law requires that the license be issued.

The author's best advice is to apply through your county sheriff's department or county police department.

Once you get the license, carry with confidence, and do it discreetly.

WHAT ABOUT 'OPEN CARRY?'

IMPORTANT! There is considerable misunderstanding, and debate, about the right of "Open Carry" in Washington state. Various legal authorities consulted by the author, including at least one major law enforcement agency, consider open carry legal, but not without limitations as spelled out in **RCW 9.41.270 (1):** *It shall be unlawful for any person to carry, exhibit, display, or draw any firearm, dagger, sword, knife or other cutting or stabbing instrument, club, or any other weapon apparently capable of producing bodily harm, in a manner, under circumstances, and at a time and place that either manifests an intent to intimidate another or that warrants alarm for the safety of other persons.*

Thus, it is essentially how others view your open carry of a firearm that is important, not necessarily your intent. If someone else is alarmed for their safety by your appearance in their proximity with a firearm carried openly, you could be charged under this statute. One former assistant prosecutor, now a legal advisor with a large metropolitan police agency, noted that "after 9-11, people are more skittish, and could be more apt to call" the police."

"A fact-finder," this attorney cautioned, "might find that fear more reasonable."

Carrying a firearm openly can quickly deteriorate into an "in your face" act, and it is the author's advice to avoid provocative conduct whenever you are armed. It's nobody's business, and you don't need to tell the whole world visually that you are carrying a gun.

This was affirmed in the case of *State V. Spencer*, in which the State Court of Appeals issued a 1994 ruling that clearly places a burden of responsibility on the gun owner *"to ascertain when the carrying of a particular weapon would reasonably warrant alarm in others."*

The defendant in this case, Randolph Spencer, was arrested by a Federal Way police officer one night in August 1991. He had been walking his dog down the street while carrying a loaded AK-47 semiautomatic rifle, by a sling over his shoulder. He was also carrying a .45-caliber pistol under his jacket, and was licensed to do so. A passing motorist saw this and reported it to some nearby firefighters, who also saw Spencer and, like the motorist, "became concerned," so they called police.

Spencer claimed a defense based on the state constitutional right to keep and bear arms provision (Article 1, Section 24), and he challenged the constitutionality of RCW 9.41.270. Both the King County Superior Court and the Appeals Court ruled against him, and the State Supreme Court let the ruling stand.

The appeals court, in discussing Article 1, Section 24, ruled, *"Although this provision is stated in absolute terms, the right to bear arms is subject to reasonable regulation by the State under its police power."*

Later in its ruling, the Appeals Court also stated that RCW 9.41.270 *"does not prevent a person from carrying weapons in self-defense. Weapons may be carried in response to 'presently threatened unlawful force by another'. RCW 9.41.270(3)(c). If there is no present threat, weapons must be carried in a manner that does not warrant alarm in others. The statute does not prohibit the ownership of weapons, and it limits the possession of certain weapons only when they are carried or displayed in a manner and under circumstances that warrant alarm. Thus, for example, the statute does not prohibit an individual from legally carrying a concealed weapon such as the .45-caliber pistol Spencer carried under his jacket. We conclude that the statute's restriction on an individual's right to bear arms in self-defense is minimal. The statute is narrowly drawn and demonstrates the Legislature's awareness of and concern with preserving the rights of the individual."*

Perhaps most important, the court stated, *"...the prohibition is not so vague that it would prevent persons of common intelligence from ever carrying a weapon on the street. In the vast majority of situations, a person of common intelligence would be able to ascertain when the carrying of a particular weapon would reasonably warrant alarm in others. Although some areas of uncertainty may exist, these potential 'gray areas' of the statute are small and do not render it unconstitutional."*

"Finally, contrary to Spencer's argument, the statute does promote public welfare and safety. People have a strong interest in being able to use public areas without fearing for their lives. The statute protects this interest by requiring people who carry weapons to do so in a manner that will not warrant alarm. Therefore, we conclude that the statute is reasonably necessary and substantially promotes the public welfare.

"To summarize, we have determined that the statute minimally restricts the rights of the individual, it is narrowly drawn, and it promotes a substantial public interest. This public interest in security, and in having a sense of security, outweighs the individual's interest in carrying weapons under circumstances that warrant alarm in others. For these reasons, we hold that the restriction in RCW 9.41.270 on the right to bear arms is not unconstitutional."

Translation: While "open carry" may be legal, it is not absolutely protected, and placing limitations on the manner of carry is not unconstitutional. The Spencer ruling places the burden of responsibility entirely on the shoulders of the gun owner to use common sense. Thus, walking down an urban street while openly carrying a loaded handgun could easily get you in legal trouble when it *"would warrant alarm in a reasonable person."* Most assuredly, strolling down a city street with a loaded rifle (or shotgun) slung over one's shoulder does not appear to be defensible conduct, as spelled out in the *Spencer* ruling.

If you carry a loaded handgun openly in a public place, whether intentionally provocative or not, it may be construed as a provocative act, and you will almost certainly be contacted by police. **Don't be stupid.**

Furthermore, don't start debating the constitution or the law with a police officer. Above all, never escalate a simple police contact into a situation where a police officer becomes fearful for his or her safety, or the safety of the general public, based on your conduct.

Concealed and Open Carry Q&A

Q. Can I carry when I go to a baseball or football game at Safeco Field or Qwest Field?

A. While these facilities have been at least partly financed with public money, they are operated by private entities, and the management bans firearms on the premises. These facilities are technically not "operated by" cities, towns, counties or other municipalities as detailed in RCW 9.41.300 (2)(b). This has yet to be challenged in court, and you should not be a test case.

Q. Can I carry when I take my kids to the state high school football, basketball and baseball tournaments if they are held at places like the Tacoma Dome?

A. No. Under RCW 9.41.280 (1), when a facility is being used exclusively by public or private schools, that facility is off limits to firearms.

Q. Is it legal for me to carry while attending sports events at the University of Washington, or other universities and colleges?

A. Every college and university in the state has its own guidelines under the Washington Administrative Code, and virtually all of them place some prohibitions on firearms. In some cases, those prohibitions apply only to students and faculty, not the public. The UW, however, has a blanket prohibition that applies to everyone. See the Appendix for further information.

Q. Can I carry while attending a function at the Washington State Convention Center over I-5 in Seattle?

A. Yes. This is a public facility, but organizations leasing all or part of the facility may set their own rules, and if a group wants to prohibit people attending its function from carrying, they may legally do so. You will still be able to carry in other parts of the facility not under the control of the leasing organization.

Q. I have a concealed pistol license. With the heightened security on Washington State Ferries, can I carry aboard a ferry?

A. Yes. State ferries are considered an extension of the state highway system, and if you are licensed to carry, you may carry aboard a ferry. Concealment is the key element, here, of course. Someone night report you if they spot your handgun, and you may be contacted by a law enforcement officer.

Q. May I carry concealed in a restaurant? What about a tavern?

A. You may legally carry in a restaurant, provided that you may **NOT** carry in the cocktail lounge section of the restaurant, which is off limits to anyone under age 21. You may **NOT** carry legally in a tavern.

Q. Can I carry concealed in a National Forest or on State Forest land?

A. Yes, your CPL is good on state and national forest lands. It is **NOT** good in a National Park, however. You may also carry in State, County and city parks. Also, under RCW 9.41.060 (8) you may carry concealed without a license if you are *"engaging in a lawful outdoor recreational activity such as hunting, fishing, camping, hiking, or horseback riding..."*

Q. Where else may I legally carry a concealed handgun without a CPL?

A. In your home or place of business, provided it is YOUR place of business, and not your workplace where you are simply an employee and workplace rules prohibit firearms.

Q. I'm licensed to carry, so why can't I carry at work?

A. Private businesses can set their own guidelines for employee conduct while on the job. If you violate these guidelines, you can be disciplined or fired, and it is not a defense to argue that you have a constitutional right to bear arms. This is a case of competing rights; the right of the employer to establish employee conduct in the workplace versus your individual right to bear arms under the state constitution.

Q. Is it legal for me to carry openly?

A. Yes and no. Washington is, theoretically, an open carry state. However, under RCW 9.41.270, armed citizens must exercise great discretion. Section (1) of that statute places restrictions on Open Carry: *"It shall be unlawful for any person to carry, exhibit, display, or draw any firearm, dagger, sword, knife or other cutting or stabbing instrument, club, or any other weapon apparently capable of producing bodily harm, in a manner, under circumstances, and at a time and place that either manifests an intent to intimidate another or that warrants alarm for the safety of other persons."* Out in the forest, when you are engaged in a lawful activity, you are good to go. In downtown Seattle or Spokane for example, you could be sacked under RCW 9.41.270. This question centers on a definition of what "warrants alarm" in another person. Under the law, this is determined solely by a subjective judgment on the part of the observer, whether a private citizen or police officer, and NOT in the intent or action of the armed citizen. There has been a test case, and he lost.

Chapter Five

USE OF FORCE

RCW 9A 16.050 Homicide - By other person - When justifiable. Homicide (by a private citizen - ed .) is also justifiable when committed either:

(1) In the lawful defense of the slayer, or his or her husband, wife, parent, child, brother, or sister, or of any other person in his presence or company, when there is reasonable ground to apprehend a design on the part of the person slain to commit a felony or to do some great personal injury to the slayer or to any such person, and there is imminent danger of such design being accomplished; or

(2) In the actual resistance of an attempt to commit a felony upon the slayer, in his presence or upon or in a dwelling, or other place of abode, in which he is (1975 lst ex.s. c 260 9A.16.050)

"The law is well settled that there is ***no duty to retreat*** *when a person is assaulted in a place where he or she has a right to be."* — Washington State Supreme Court, Nov. 6, 2003, *State of Washington V Reynaldo Redmond,* 72910-7

When the Washington State Supreme Court reaffirmed that there is no duty to retreat from an imminent threat in the 2003 case of *State V. Reynaldo Redmond,* it was reinforcing an important 1999 ruling in the case of *State v. Studd* in which the defendant had shot a person who was holding him at gunpoint. The state high court held, in *Studd,* that *"retreat was not a reasonable alternative to the use of force for a person being held at gunpoint."* The court further noted that, in the event a citizen is prosecuted after having used deadly force against another — and who claims self-defense — the trial court *"cannot allow the defendant to put forth a theory of self-defense, yet refuse to provide corresponding jury instructions that are supported by the evidence in the case."*

This is a landmark concept, and while the "no duty to retreat" doctrine is not unique to Washington State, it is not a universal legal principle. Other jurisdictions do require citizens to demonstrate that they had retreated from a threat, and exhausted the retreat option. In Washington, when a person is *"assaulted in a place where he or she has a right to be"* the assaulted person may stand his or her ground.

This is especially so in *"a dwelling, or other place of abode, in which he is."* This includes your residence, another person's residence where you are an invited guest, or the home of a relative, for example. It might also include a hotel or motel room, or even a campsite on public or private land where you have a legitimate right to be.

Even though written several years prior to both the *Studd* and *Redmond* cases, the his landmark self-defense book *In the Gravest Extreme*, author Massad

Ayoob accurately sums up the spirit, and intent, of Washington State's self-defense statute by noting that "American laws universally condone homicide only when undertaken to escape imminent and unavoidable danger of death or grave bodily harm."

Ayoob's use of the term "escape" does not mean that the individual needs to be retreating from a deadly threat, only that the citizen acting in self-defense be acting to defend himself from the imminent and unavoidable threat.

Washington state law regarding the use of lethal force in self defense might best be described as founded on what is commonly called the "Reasonable Man Doctrine." This translates to taking an action that any reasonable and prudent person would have taken, in the same situation, knowing what you knew at the time.

Remember these words, from RCW 9A.16.050: *"....when there is reasonable ground to apprehend a design....."* What this means in layman's terms is when it is "reasonable to conclude an intent" on the part of the person against whom you use lethal force.

Be careful here. It may not be considered good enough at an inquest or in a court trial that you had reason to assume (Remember, when you "assume," you make an Ass out of U and Me....) but it can be argued that you fired because you concluded beyond any doubt that to do otherwise would have resulted in grave bodily harm or death to you or another person.

Translation: The judgment of a reasonable man or woman.

'NECESSARY AND REASONABLE'

Long before anyone starts drawing guns and shooting, a thorough look at Washington's statutes regarding the use of force must take place.

Under the provisions of RCW 9A.16.020, it is lawful to use force under six scenarios, which cover force used by both law enforcement officers and private citizens. This section does not apply to the use of lethal force, but force other than lethal force.

(1) Whenever necessarily used by a public officer in the performance of a legal duty, or a person assisting the officer and acting under the officer's direction:

(2) Whenever necessarily used by a person arresting one who has committed a felony and delivering him or her to a public officer competent to receive him or her into custody; (This refers to an act commonly called "citizen's arrest" and unless it is an extreme case the armed private citizen is well advised not to try this because of the immediate physical and long-term legal consequences.)

(3) Whenever used by a party about to be injured, or by another lawfully aiding him or her, in preventing or attempting to prevent an offense against his or her person, or a malicious trespass, or other malicious interference with

real or personal property lawfully in his or her possession, in case the force is not more than is necessary.

(This leads us into the area of "equal force" and "disparity of force." Essentially, you cannot use force greater than that which is used against you, i.e., if someone pushes you, you may not respond by drawing a gun and firing.)

(4) Whenever reasonably used by a person to detain someone who enters or remains unlawfully in a building or on real property lawfully in the possession of such person, so long as such detention is reasonable in duration and manner to investigate the reason for the detained person's presence on the premises, and so long as the premises in question did not reasonably appear to be intended to be open to members of the public;

"In the event an armed citizen takes the life of a criminal, there will be an investigation by the police, a coroner's inquest and possibly a criminal trial."

(5) Whenever used by a carrier of passengers or the carrier's authorized agent or servant, or other person assisting them at their request in expelling from a carriage, railway car, vessel, or other vehicle, a passenger who refuses to obey a lawful and reasonable regulation prescribed for the conduct of passengers, if such vehicle has first been stopped and the force used is not more than is necessary to expel the offender with reasonable regard to the offender's personal safety;

(6) Whenever used by any person to prevent a mentally ill, mentally incompetent, or mentally disabled person from committing an act dangerous to any person, or in enforcing necessary restraint for the protection or restoration to health of the person during such period only as is necessary to obtain legal authority for the restraint or custody of the person.

Did you count the number of times the word "reasonable" or a variation was used? Four.

Washington State law on the use of deadly force has a curious— some might argue questionable — quirk. There is a double standard, one for peace officers and persons aiding them, and another for private citizens acting in their own defense or in the defense of a third innocent party.

When the State Legislature passed RCW 9A.16.040 in 1986, which addresses justifiable homicide or the use of deadly force by public officers, peace officers or persons aiding, clearly rec-ognized that double standard, and inserted language in the state statutes to that effect:

"Legislative recognition: The legislature recognizes that RCW 9A.16.040 establishes a dual standard with respect to the use of deadly force by peace officers and private citizens, and further recognizes that private citizens permissible use of deadly force under the authority of RCW 9.01.200, 9A.16.020 or 9A.16.050 is not restricted and remains broader than the limitations imposed on peace officers."

In short, by legislative decree, private citizens have somewhat greater latitude in the use of deadly force than commissioned peace officers.

However, do not misunderstand, nor take for granted, this provision. RCW 9A.16.040 is not a declaration by the Legislature that the armed private citizen enjoys an open season on criminal suspects.

As explained at the beginning of this chapter, the armed private citizen may only resort to the use of deadly force within the bounds of reasonableness, as defined in RCW 9A.16.050.

In the event an armed private citizen is forced by circumstances to take the life of a criminal, there will most certainly be an investigation by the police, a coroner's inquest and possibly a criminal trial.

Do yourself a big favor. Get an attorney. That's the extent of the author's legal advice on the subject. Now for the good news.

Washington law also offers one more interesting curio, quite possibly unique to the state. It's RCW 9A.16.110, previously known as RCW 9.01.200. This is the chapter that requires the state to indemnify or reimburse a defendant who is found not guilty of homicide by reason of self defense, for all reasonable costs.

So states the chapter, in part: *"When a substantial question of self defense in such a case shall exist which needs legal investigation or court action for the full determination of the facts, and the defendant's actions are subsequently found justified under the intent of this section, the state of Washington shall indemnify or reimburse such defendant for all loss of time, legal fees, or other expenses involved in his or her defense."*

This indemnification *"is an award of reasonable costs which include loss of time, legal fees, or other expenses and is not an independent cause of action."* This could include expert witness fees, independent investigation fees, etc. For the complete text of this section, turn to the Appendix.

There is yet another protection for the armed private citizen, this one covering those rare instances when the citizen is aiding a peace officer. It's RCW 9.01.055, entitled "Citizen immunity if aiding officer, scope - When."

"Private citizens aiding a police officer, or other officers of the law in the performance of their duties as police officers or officers of the law, shall have the same civil and criminal immunity as such officer, as a result of any act or commission for aiding or attempting to aid a police officer or other officer of the law, when such officer is in imminent danger of loss of life or grave bodily injury or when such officer requests such assistance and when such action was taken under emergency conditions and in good faith."

Here, again, the armed private citizen must act with the utmost prudence. Drawing your licensed concealed weapon should be the very last move you want to make, not the first.

Though the language of the law appears to grant the armed private citizen certain immunities, bear in mind that your actions will most definitely come under the same scrutiny as the actions of any peace officer who is compelled to employ deadly force.

It is wise to obtain legal counsel in anticipation of any such situation.

COMMON QUESTIONS ABOUT SELF-DEFENSE

The use of deadly force requires much consideration, and unfortunately, split-second decisiveness. We are not going to launch into a discussion about tactics. Here, we will merely discuss some of the practical ramifications.

Q. If I am attacked in my home, or on my property and I am in imminent danger of grave bodily harm or death, must I make an effort to flee before defending myself?

A. No. The Washington State Supreme Court has clearly ruled in at least two important cases, *State v. Studd* and *State v. Reynaldo Redmond* that when faced with an imminent threat or an attack that is already under way, *"The law is well settled that there is no duty to retreat when a person is assaulted in a place where he or she has a right to be."*

Consider that a reasonable person would certainly take whatever opportunity possible to call 911 for police assistance — provided there is time to do so without placing yourself in jeopardy — but such a call for help is not required when the attack is imminent, and most assuredly not required if an attack has already commenced. After all, no criminal is going to stop in the midst of his attack and allow you to call the police, then wait for them to arrive.

Do not confuse the language in *Studd* or *Redmond* to encourage unsafe or unnecessary heroics. Foolishly placing one's self in jeopardy is not the same thing as defending one's self in the face of an imminent attack or one that has already commenced.

Q. What if an attack occurs while I am staying at a motel, or camping in a state or national forest, or at the beach, or even on private land where I have permission to camp? What about in a public place, like a shopping mall, grocery store, restaurant or parking lot?

A. A motel room, a campsite where you are staying for the night, or even longer, is traditionally considered your temporary place of abode and you have, as observed by the State Supreme Court, "a right to be" there. In such a venue, the private citizen is within his or her rights of self-defense if attacked. In a public place, your right of self-defense remains. The *Redmond* case involved self-defense in a public place, the parking lot of a high school. This was not a deadly force confrontation, but one involving the use of less-than-lethal force in self-defense.

A word to the wise: The assault or life-threatening attack cannot be provoked. That is, at no time can you be a willing participant in actions that escalate to the use of lethal force. See next question.

Q. When does a self-defense argument become invalid?

A. At the point you become a willing participant to any action that escalates to, and culminates in, your use of deadly force, you cannot claim self-defense. If you are confronted by some jerk in a restaurant, cocktail lounge or other social setting, the correct response would be to ask that he leave you alone (loud enough so witnesses can hear), ask the management or your host to intervene, or simply leave. Once you challenge this bozo to step outside and square off, forget about any self-defense plea should you end up seriously injuring or killing your tormenter.

More important, if you deliberately provoke an attack, it might easily be argued that the individual who strikes back, or even strikes first, was acting in self-defense against you.

Q. If I am confronted by someone threatening me with a knife, is it legal for me to shoot him?

A. Readers should recall the David Walker incident in Seattle in early 2000. Seattle Police shot and killed Walker, a suspect in an armed robbery, who was skipping down a sidewalk, waving a knife and ignoring repeated commands to stop and drop the knife. The entire incident was recorded by a television news photographer. Immediately before the fatal shot was fired, Walker made a threatening gesture by raising the knife above his head.

Armed private citizens faced with a similar situation should note research conducted by now-retired Salt Lake City, Utah police Lt. Dennis Tueller. He determined in 1982 that an individual armed with a knife could cross a distance of 21 feet in under two seconds, less time than it takes a police officer to react, draw his sidearm and fire. A knife-wielding individual who is within 21 feet can rush at you and stab you, or another innocent person, to death.

Your assailant does not need to be armed specifically with a knife. Screwdrivers, crowbars, baseball bats, hatchets, axes; virtually any object that could be used as a weapon fall within the parameters of what has become known in shooting circles as "the Tueller principle."

Remember the language found in RCW 9A.16.050, which justifies homicide by a private citizen "*... when there is reasonable ground to apprehend a design on the part of the person slain to commit a felony or to do some great personal injury to the slayer or to any such person, and there is imminent danger of such design being accomplished.*"

Q. If I find myself in the presence of a criminal act, should I intervene?

A. This is a serious judgment call that must be made with each individual situation. There is no right or wrong answer, and pontificating with a lot of

"What ifs" will do you no good. If you find yourself in a situation where you have reasonably concluded that imminent and unavoidable deadly force is about to be used against you or another innocent person, or if the attack is already underway, you are within your legal right to act in self defense, or in defense of others, especially considering the language in the Studd and Redmond decisions. You are, however, under no legal obligation to intervene. If you do intervene, be absolutely certain who is the perpetrator and who is the victim.

Q. Should I shoot at someone who is running out my door with my television set, stereo or other objects?

A. No. Unless a suspect has just — in your presence — committed an act of such a heinous nature that it is reasonable to conclude his continued freedom is a threat to the public at large, don't shoot, as he poses no immediate threat to your safety. Stealing your television set does not constitute a heinous crime, and the suspect's flight from the scene does not place you in jeopardy of attack. However, someone running down the street hacking at people with machete, or throwing fire bombs, or shooting up a fast food establishment or shopping mall can certainly draw a considerably different response from a reasonable person who happens to be legally armed.

Q. If I shoot someone who subsequently falls dead outside my home, should I drag him back inside?

A. Absolutely not! The author has heard police officers, even one attorney, offer this kind of advice to homeowners. This constitutes a criminal act, tampering with evidence, and the investigating police officers will certainly discover it right away. It will be no defense for the armed private citizen to try and excuse himself/herself by explaining: "Well, a cop told me to do it!" By the same token, if you do it, then lie about it, you're going to have to continue lying, and when you get caught in the lie (I didn't say "if"), you will be in big trouble, because there goes your credibility with investigators. (Besides, do you really want to touch someone whom you've just shot, and possibly killed, because he was trying to do the same to you? Do you want his bloodstains all over your carpet?)

Q. Can I shoot someone through a door?

A. You're on shaky ground, unless it can be clearly demonstrated that you had reasonably concluded the suspect was about to crash through the door and would have caused you grave bodily harm or death had he done so. (By the time this happens, you should have already been on the telephone to the police, and — barring the eventuality that the intruder has cut your telephone wires — they are still on the phone, and an officer is en route.)

Q. Can I shoot to prevent certain crimes?

A. We're right back to the parameters of RCW 9A.16.050 "*... when there is reasonable ground to apprehend a design on the part of the person slain to commit a felony or to do some great personal injury...*"

For example, you're aroused in the middle of the night by a commotion outside. You investigate and find someone preparing to set fire to your house, perhaps with a lighted molotov cocktail still in hand. Can you shoot? Well, what would any reasonable person do in the same situation, knowing what you know at the time?

Include under this question the following crimes for which a lethal force intervention may be justified: First or second degree murder, sexual assault, arson of an occupied structure, kidnapping and armed robbery.

Q. Should I follow a suspect outside my home and fire as he flees?

A. Absolutely not, even if he's been shooting at you. Once he runs, let him go. Apprehension is strictly in the realm of trained police officers, not an adrenalin-charged armed private citizen. You must never take a gunfight into the street, as you could be legally liable for whatever happens as a result. A gunfight in the street is not contained; loose bullets can, and do fly in just about every direction. Innocent bystanders are placed in harm's way, even if it's 3 a.m. and your bullet sails a hundred yards and penetrates the wall of a slumbering neighbor's house.

Q. What should I do if I am involved in a shooting, regardless whether anyone is wounded or killed?

A. You should IMMEDIATELY call the police if you had not already done so when it appeared a violent confrontation was imminent. In the event you have fired at someone and he flees, you need to be the first person to dial 911, because if you do not, there is always the possibility that the person you fired at will call police and file a complaint against you out of revenge.

You need to provide information that the call receiver asks for. Remember, for those who are not medical doctors, do not suddenly try to become one while speaking on the telephone with the 911 operator. You should advise the call receiver that there has been a shooting at your location, advise the call receiver that you are armed, what you are wearing and where you are. If someone has been wounded, say so, and the 911 operator will dispatch an aid car.

When the police arrive, do what they tell you, first time, every time, or risk getting arrested or shot. When the aid car arrives, stay out of the way.

Remember, you have the right to remain silent. When police officers are involved in a shooting, they may decline to give a statement until after they have consulted with legal counsel and you are entitled to the same consideration.

Whatever statements you make to the police, don't embellish, don't exaggerate, don't ramble, and don't lie.

Q. What if I only display the firearm and do not fire a shot? Should I still call the police?

A. Absolutely, and do it fast, before your would-be attacker has the opportunity to call in a complaint about the nut who just threatened him with a gun. Provide a description of the suspect, and be sure to make it clear that you will press charges and be willing to testify in court.

The only time you should display a firearm is when it is reasonable to conclude you are in imminent and unavoidable danger of grave bodily harm or death.

Q. Where can I get competent training in the use of firearms for self protection?

A. Contact a National Rifle Association-certified personal protection instructor for basic training. For advanced instruction, there are several options including the Firearms Academy of Seattle or Insights Training Center. Care to travel? Try the Lethal Force Institute, Concord, N.H.; Gunsite Training Center, Paulden, Ariz.; Chapman Academy, Hallsville, Mo., or Thunder Ranch, Lakeview, Ore.

A word to the wise. Firearms training is a good thing. Lots of training and frequent practice are better.

There are, however, two ways that lots of training might be perceived. On the one hand, you might be considered an upstanding citizen, investing much time and personal finances into improving your skill, and judgment, with firearms.

But on the other hand, "lots" of training (i.e., reasonable training, practice, etc.) might easily be portrayed as excessive training by a politically-motivated prosecutor, and understood as such by an easily-swayed jury. Do not put unwavering faith in juries, especially in the wake of Rodney King II, or the first Menendez and Simpson trials.

Be very prudent about attending courses that could leave you easily labeled as a paranoid in constant need of a machismo fix, or some sort of "Dirty Harry" wannabe. Select a good shooting school, and stick with it.

Popular Shooting Schools

Lethal Force Institute

P.O. Box 122
Concord, NH 03302-0122
(603) 224-6814

The Chapman Academy

4350 Academy Road
Hallsville, MO 65255
(573) 696-5544

Thunder Ranch

96747 HWY 140 East
Lakeview, OR 97630
(541) 947-4104

Firearms Academy of Seattle

P.O. Box 400
Onalaska, WA 98570
(360) 978-6100

Gunsite Training Center

P.O. Box 700
Paulden, AZ 86334
(520) 636-4565

Insights Training Center

P.O. Box 3585
Bellevue, WA 98009-3585
(425) 739-0133

For Basic Instruction:

The National Rifle Association

11250 Waples Mill Road
Fairfax, VA 22030
(703) 267-1000

Chapter Six
LONG GUNS

Since the federal National Instant Check System (NICS) provision of the Brady Law took effect, all firearms purchases require such a "check." The dealer calls the NICS headquarters for clearance to transfer the firearm, and if clearance is confirmed, the transfer can take place. This applies to rifle and shotgun purchases, but there is no waiting period on long guns beyond that required to successfully complete the background check.

Federal statute allows the purchase and possession of long guns by persons over the age of 18 years (Title 18 U.S.C., § 922 (b)(1)).

Such rifles and shotguns, of course, must comply with state and federal law. That is, they must be exempt from the federal ban on the future manufacture of 19 types (make that 185 known firearms and their look-alikes) of so-called "assault rifles" and be legal under state law.

Under federal law, rifles must have barrels in excess of 16 inches, and shotguns must have barrels in excess of 18 inches.

It is not necessary to obtain any kind of permit to purchase a rifle or shotgun, nor must a permit be acquired in order to transport. You must still fill out Federal form 4473.

Remember, you may not purchase or be in possession of any firearm if you have been convicted of certain misdemeanors and all felonies, including domestic violence, or if you are under indictment.

You may not possess or purchase a firearm if you are under a domestic violence restraining order under the provisions of the Violence Against Women Act of 1994 (the federal statute under which Texas physician Timothy Joe Emerson was convicted; see Chapter 1.).

You can carry a rifle or shotgun freely on rural public land where not prohibited by special regulations. During the hunting season, of course, be sure to have a hunting license and to obey all the game regulations, as spelled out in the annual Hunting Regulations and Big Game Seasons pamphlet. And take special note that in order to shoot any live game or varmints, you must have a state hunting license.

Shotguns and rifles may be kept in the home or primary place of business for personal protection.

They may not be openly carried for that purpose, other than on your private property. Repeal of the "open carry" prohibition in RCW 9.41.050 only allows unloaded long guns to be carried uncased on window racks or elsewhere in vehicles.

Gun owners are reminded that the Washington RCW 77.15.460 specifically prohibits carrying a loaded rifle or shotgun in or on any motor vehicle. It should be noted that the placement of any loaded rifle or shotgun on any part of a vehicle at any time, even the act of laying a rifle in the open bed of a pickup truck, or leaning a loaded rifle or shotgun against a vehicle, can draw a citation from a wildlife enforcement agent or other law enforcement officer.

SAFE STORAGE

It is strongly recommended that rifles and shotguns be stored unloaded, with their actions open, in a locked case, security cabinet or gun safe. Ammunition should be stored separately.

Where home defense is concerned, the use of a high-powered rifle is discouraged because of their inherent "over-penetration" capabilities. A high-powered rifle bullet will typically shoot through any intruder, penetrate interior walls and possibly exit the abode, causing injury to someone outside, or even penetrate the walls of another residence, injuring someone there.

Shotguns, on the other hand, pose less a dilemma, depending upon how they are loaded. Magnum Double-0 buckshot will penetrate interior walls and even exit through exterior walls. This is not necessarily so with a charge of birdshot, but you should be aware that a charge of birdshot, fired at ranges typical of interior room distance, will still be extremely tight, constituting a mass about the size of a softball. Such a mass can penetrate and pass through interior walls.

However, shotguns are substantial home defense firearms, and sometimes preferred by private citizens because of their power, versatility and because they are not handguns.

To legally purchase a rifle or shotgun under federal and state law, you must fill out a federal Form 4473. This form asks several questions about your criminal history, mental health background, nationality and drug use. It is a violation of federal law to answer any of these questions with false information.

Earlier, it was noted that there is no waiting period or background check for the purchase of a rifle or shotgun by a Washington resident who is legally allowed to own a firearm.

Again, under the federal Brady Law, a national instant background check system is now in place, requiring everyone who purchases a firearm from a federally licensed dealer to go through a background check. But, again, there is no waiting period on the purchase of a rifle or shotgun.

Chapter Seven
TRAVELING WITH FIREARMS

Under the federal McClure-Volkmer Act (also called the Firearm Owner Protection Act), passed in 1986, private citizens may travel with firearms legally in the U.S., provided they obey certain provisions of the law.

In the simplest terms, you are allowed to take a firearm from one state to another in a private vehicle so long as you may legally own that firearm in your home state and the state to which you are traveling. It must be unloaded, and locked in the trunk. In vehicles without a trunk, it must be in a locked compartment (other than the glove box or console), in an area not immediately accessible to the passenger area.

Be forewarned, however, that in certain jurisdictions, personalized vanity license plates or even window decals that indicate you are a hunter, shooter or member of the National Rifle Association or some hunting organization, occasionally may make the local police take a harder look at your vehicle. They will look for any violation that would justify a stop leading to an inquiry about any firearms you may be transporting or carrying for legitimate purposes.

As noted in Chapter 4, if you are pulled over, you are under no legal obligation to immediately inform a police officer if there is a firearm in your vehicle. If you travel to another state to go hunting, be smart and don't drive in your hunting clothes. If you are so stupid as to drink and drive with an open beer can in your lap, you deserve to be arrested, lose your guns, possibly your vehicle, maybe even your driver's license. You deserve no sympathy.

CARRYING CONCEALED IN VEHICLE

Within the borders of Washington state, anyone licensed to carry a concealed handgun may have that firearm loaded, and on his/her person, while traveling by private vehicle.

Exceptions: Concealed carry permits are not valid inside National Parks or on military reservations, any federal courthouse or Post Office building. All of this was discussed in Chapter Four.

Remember: A Washington concealed carry license is valid only inside the state borders, and in 18 other states as of this writing. It is not valid in neighboring Oregon (where non-resident CPLs are available) and most definitely not California.

It is, however, valid in Alaska, Arizona, Idaho, Kentucky, Indiana, Louisiana, Michigan, Mississippi, Missouri, Montana, North Carolina, Ohio, Oklahoma, South Dakota, Tennessee, Texas, Utah, and Virginia. The author has carried concealed in Michigan and Kentucky on my Washington CPL with no problem. I also have a Florida CPL, which allows me to carry in several other states.

Note that in Vermont, there is no CPL, but open and concealed carry are allowed under a century-old State Supreme Court ruling, provided the firearm is not carried with the intent to harm another person. In Alaska, open and concealed carry are also allowed without a CPL, although Alaska continues to issue resident CPLs for the purpose of enabling its citizens to carry in other states.

If traveling in other states and carrying concealed, be certain to study that state's laws regarding concealed carry in advance, so that you carry in compliance with their regulations. Visit **www.packing.org** for updates

If you are carrying concealed in a vehicle in another state, be prepared to display your CPL immediately to an officer if you are pulled over in a traffic stop. In Washington State, you are not required to display your CPL until or unless the officer asks to see it.

AIRLINE TRAVEL

Since the horrendous Sept. 11, 2001 terrorist attack on this country, restrictions on airline travel have tightened significantly. However, at the time of this writing, it appears that travel with firearms will continue under the federal regulations that were in place before that horrible Tuesday.

Under Federal Air Regulation 107.21(a), administered by the Federal Aviation Administration, "*...no person may have an explosive, incendiary, or deadly or dangerous weapon on or about the individual's person or accessible property.*"

Simply put, you may not fly with a firearm on your person, nor may you carry a gun on board a commercial aircraft in your carry-on luggage. No exceptions. You can't "check it with the pilot," and you will never smuggle the gun through the security checkpoint.

Also, the airlines are subject to the same federal firearms regulations. Federal Air Regulation 108.11(2)(d), which covers carrying weapons aboard aircraft, says airlines may not "*...knowingly permit any person to transport, nor may any person transport or tender for transport any unloaded firearm in checked baggage aboard an airplane unless:*

(1) The passenger declares to the certificate holder, either orally or in writing before checking the baggage, that any firearm carried in the baggage is unloaded;

(2) The firearm is carried in a container the certificate holder considers appropriate for air transportation;

(3) When the firearm is other than a shotgun or rifle, or other firearm normally fired from the shoulder position, the baggage in which it is carried is locked, and only the passenger checking the baggage retains the key or combination; and

(4) The baggage containing the firearm is carried in an area other than the flight crew compartment that is inaccessible to passengers."

Flying with firearms, especially handguns, can be a hassle. There is the ever-present danger of theft or breakage of a valuable gun. Then there is dealing with ticket agents who can hassle you where it is not warranted. In such cases, immediately ask for a supervisor.

You must declare all firearms when checking in at the main terminal. Under no circumstances will you be permitted to take a firearm through a carry-on baggage checkpoint, so don't even try.

Whenever traveling with firearms, arrive at the airport early. Waiting in line takes time and checking a firearm can take several minutes.

The gun case must be of the lockable variety. You can then tuck it unobtrusively into your hard or soft luggage, or a duffel bag, which may, or may not, be locked. It is prudent to lock your outer case, also. You're being foolish if you don't.

The ticket agent may ask to check the firearm to see that it is unloaded. This is acceptable, and within their authority. Comply with as little commotion as possible (only an idiot would wave a gun around inside an airport terminal!), then lock the case. You will be asked to fill out a tag (tan, white or orange) that bears the words: "Firearms unloaded," with the date and your signature. You may then place the tag inside your gun case or luggage, so it is not visible.

With long guns, it's another matter. If you can break your shotgun or rifle down into two pieces, and travel with them in a short case, do it. It is the long gun cases that simply cannot be disguised as something they are not. Even with the orange tag stuffed inside, that gun case screams to one and all: "Yep, there's a gun in here!"

NOTE: The "firearms unloaded" tag is not specifically required by law. Essentially, by asking for the tag and filling it out, you are declaring the presence of a firearm to the baggage handler, and assuring him/her that the gun is packaged as required by regulation, in a lockable case.

With the tag inside and out of sight, see your luggage slide onto the belt, then get to your gate of departure quickly.

Why? So you can be assured that your luggage actually makes it into the plane's luggage hold. Many times, travel-wary shooters have thwarted airport gun theft with such a strategy. The author carries a small pair of binoculars in carry-on luggage, just for this purpose. If your case doesn't show up, inform the gate attendant immediately, and request that airport security check on your luggage at once. It is your legal right, and responsibility, to do so.

You may not have ammunition for the firearm in the gun case, so pack it separately, and be sure it is stored in its original container or a hard container.

If flying into a foreign country, check well in advance with local authorities about their firearms laws. In Canada, for example, traveling with handguns is strictly regulated, and so is traveling with certain types of long guns (black guns with folding stocks, for example, are frowned upon). Under new Canadian regulations, visitors must register all guns.

Declare your firearms at airports, and when you travel in Canada, firearms must be unloaded and locked. Take a trigger lock along, put the trigger lock on the gun, and lock the gun inside the case.

Incidentally, since Canada is our most immediate foreign neighbor, Washington citizens should be forewarned that Canada's Parliament has enacted arguably the most draconian federal gun law in the modern world. It is primarily aimed at Canadian citizens, but should you, a citizen of the U.S., run afoul of this law, you are not protected by our state or federal constitutions.

If traveling to other countries, be doubly sure about their national gun laws. In some nations, particularly in the Far East, you can go to jail for a very long time, and your Constitutional rights as a U.S. citizen are of no importance if you are found in violation of a gun law, and that can include mere possession.

If you are going on a hunting trip, your guide and outfitter will have all the necessary information on travel with firearms in his state or country. Follow his advice to the letter and don't start making up your own rules along the way.

One final note. These days, ticket agents are required to ask each passenger if they personally packed their luggage, and whether they have been asked to check or carry any luggage or parcel on board that is not their own. They will also request a photo I.D. (a driver's license suffices). It may seem silly, but it's to insure your safety.

Take some advice from a veteran traveler: *NEVER* let a stranger handle your baggage, and *NEVER* agree to carry a package or luggage that is not yours. If some stranger approaches you and asks that you carry their bags, refuse and report it to a ticket agent immediately.

Last but certainly not least. Do not joke about guns, knives, bombs or hijackings. My personal philosophy about the wisdom, or lack thereof, in requiring airline passengers to essentially leave their right of self-defense at the airline ticket counter, the author has what might best be called a very low to non-existent B.S. tolerance level on the subject of airport jokes, and absolutely no sense of humor, especially since that awful Sept. 11. Neither do airport police or federal authorities.

CARRYING IN OTHER STATES

Here is a brief overview of the requirements Washington residents will face when they carry under their Washington CPLs in other states that recognize our license, or in Vermont, where no license is required. Even if not specifically mentioned below, you may not carry concealed in any federal office building or federal government facility.

ALASKA: Alaska is the first state to pass legislation allowing open or concealed carry without a license. Thus, within the state, no license is required to carry a firearm openly or concealed. Alaska continues to recognize the Washington CPL. When contacted by a peace officer, you must immediately advise the officer that you are carrying a concealed handgun and are licensed to do so. You may not carry concealed in a residence unless you get permission to do so, and you may not carry anywhere possession of a handgun is prohibited under state or federal law.

The standard prohibition against carry in federal buildings also applies.

ARIZONA: Arizona is an open carry state. As long as a portion of the holster is visible, the handgun is not concealed. You may not carry in any establishment licensed to serve alcohol for on-premises consumption. Firearms are also prohitibed on public school grounds (other than parking lots), state colleges and universities, polling places on election day, correctional facilities (including parking lots), commercial nuclear or hydroelectric facilities and establishments open to the public where the management/owner either provides safe storage or asks you to remove the firearm from the premises. Some Indian reservations allow concealed carry, others do not. Check www.packing.org for details.

There is no requirement to inform a peace officer you are carrying, but you mist present a CPL upon request.

IDAHO: You may not carry on school property unless it is part of an authorized program or function. You may have one in your vehicle while dropping off or picking up a student.

You may not carry in a courthouse, juvenile detention center, jail, public or private school.

The license must be on your person at all times you are carrying.

INDIANA: Licenses issued by other states or foreign countries are recognized according to the terms thereof, but only while the person holding the license is not a resident of Indiana.

You may not carry on school grounds or in federal facilities, prisons or jails. You may also not carry in airports or on airplanes, and some locations, such as taverns and cocktail lounges may be restricted by the posting of proper signage (i.e., "No firearms allowed in this establishment") and possibly hospitals and courthouses, by local ordinance.

Be advised that Indiana statute allows for local municipalities to set emergency firearms regulations.

KENTUCKY: You must have the license with you at all times you are carrying a firearm, and you shall display that license upon request of a law enforcement officer.

You may not carry into a police station or sheriff's office, prison or jail, courthouse, any meeting of a government body, General Assembly or one of its committees, or any portion of an establishment licensed to dispense beer or alcoholic beverages for consumption on the premises, which portion of the establishment is primarily devoted to that purpose.

You may also not carry on elementary or secondary school grounds, in an airport beyond the security checkpoint and anywhere that carrying firearms is prohibited by federal law.

LOUISIANA: You may not carry inside a law enforcement facility. detention facility, prison or jail, courthouse or courtroom, a polling place, a meeting place of the governing authority of a political subdivision, any portion of an airport facility where carrying firearms is prohibited by federal law, or any church, synagogue, mosque or similar place of worship. You may also not carry inside any establishment that sells alcoholic beverages for on-premises consumption, and you may not carry in any school "firearm free zone." It is legal to carry a loaded firearm inside a motor vehicle.

MICHIGAN: According to the Michigan Criminal Justice Information Center, "Michigan will honor a license issued by another state as long as the pistol is carried in conformance with restrictions appearing on the license. You are afforded the same privileges allowed in your state of residency."

Michigan does not allow concealed carry on school grounds, day care centers, sports arenas or stadiums; a dining room, lounge, or bar area of a premises licensed to serve alcoholic beverages, any property or facilities owned by a church, synagogue, mosque, temple or other place of worship unless officials permit the carrying of concealed pistols on the premises.

Concealed carry is also prohibited at "entertainment facilities" with seating capacities of 2,500 or more, in hospitals, dormitories or classrooms of colleges and universities.

MISSISSIPPI: Concealed carry is not allowed in state or local police stations, jails, schools, public parks, schools, colleges, professional athletic events, any portion of an establishment, licensed to dispense alcoholic beverages for consumption on the premises, that is primarily devoted to dispensing alcoholic beverages; any portion of an establishment in which beer or light wine is consumed on the premises, that is primarily devoted to such purpose, airport passenger terminals, federal buildings and posted private facilities.

MISSOURI: Licensed citizens may not carry into jails, government buildings, amusement parks, sports arenas that hold more than 5,000 people, or schools, churches or other facilities.

MONTANA: You may not carry into buildings owned or leased by the federal, state or local government, financial institutions or rooms where alcoholic beverages are served or sold. You may also not carry in school buildings.

NORTH CAROLINA: Concealed carry is prohibited in all schools, state buildings, assemblies where admission is charged, parades, demonstrations, funeral processions, picket lines, establishments where alcohol is both sold and consumed, areas of emergency or riots, law enforcement or correctional facilities, and private property that is posted against concealed carry.

OHIO: Open carry is permitted under the Ohio State Constitution. Concealed carry is prohibited in local, county and state law enforcement facilities, jails and correctional institutions, schools, courthouses or buildings housing court facilities, places of worship, day care facilities, any and all areas of buildings leased by the state or any subdivision of the state, public or private colleges or universities (guns may be locked in cars in parking lots), airport passenger terminals, and any area where concealed carry is prohibited by federal law.

OKLAHOMA: Your firearm must remain fully concealed from detection and view. Upon coming in contact with any peace officer of this state, the person discloses the fact that he or she is in possession of a concealed firearm pursuant to a valid concealed carry weapons permit or license issued in another state. Concealed carry is prohibited in any government owned or leased buildings, at public meetings, schools, including vocational/technical institutes, jails and detention facilities, sports arenas during sporting events, any place where pari-mutual betting is allowed.

SOUTH DAKOTA: You may not carry in any establishment licensed to sell alcoholic beverages or malt beverage if that establishment derives more than half of its gross income from the sale of such beverages. You may also not carry in federal buildings, courthouses or in elementary or secondary schools, or vehicles owned by those schools. You must display your CPL upon demand by a law enforcement officer.

TENNESSEE: The permittee shall have the permit in the holder's immediate possession at all times when carrying a handgun and shall display the permit on demand of a law enforcement officer. You must have your permit on your person at all times when carrying a handgun, open or concealed.

Concealed carry is prohibited in public or private schools and campuses (guns may be locked in vehicles), school buses, on the grounds of any playground, public park, civic center or other facility or property owned, operated or used for recreational purposes; any building where alcohol is sold and consumed on the premises, and any room in which a judicial proceeding is in process.

TEXAS: You may not carry in a business that derives 51 percent or more of its gross income from the sale or on-premises consumption of alcoholic beverages. Carry is also forbidden at correctional facilities, public or private schools or educational institutions, in facilities where high school, collegiate or professional sporting events are taking place; in polling places on election day, at racetracks, the secure area of airports, in churches, synagogues or other places of worship, in hospitals, nursing homes, amusement parks and other public or private premises posted off limits to firearms as required by state law.

If you are asked for your identification by a law enforcement officer, you must immediately advise the officer that you are armed, by displaying your CPL.

UTAH: If you are stopped by a police officer and are carrying, you MUST notify the officer immediately that you are carrying a concealed firearm. You may not carry concealed into federal buildings or an airport terminal. You should also not carry onto school grounds. You may carry into a drinking establishment. However, you may not be intoxicated and in possession of a concealed handgun.

You may obtain a Utah concealed carry license, provided you meet the qualifications.

VERMONT: You may carry openly or concealed without a license provided you have no intent to injure another person.

You may not carry in any state institution or on any grounds owned or leased by that institution.

It is unlawful to carry on school grounds or in a courthouse.

VIRGINIA: You may not carry in any establishment where liquor is served, but you are allowed to carry in public buildings, including the state capitol building, under current interpretation.

Chapter Eight
HOLSTERS...AND COMMON SENSE

The author of this book is a custom concealment holster maker. I designed the original "tuckable" style holster, now marketed by my company, D&D Gunleather (P.O. Box 1638, North Bend, WA 98045), as "The UNDERSHIRT" and beautifully rendered by Mitch Rosen Extraordinary Gunleather of Manchester, N.H. as "The Workman."

It is, of course, copied in one form or another by many other holster makers.

I personally build The UNDERSHIRT holster, plus traditional Inside-the-Waist-Band (IWB) holsters and one unique belt holster called "The Flash." Simply put, I know a bit about holsters and concealed carry.

I also understand a little bit about human nature, specifically that some people carry their concealed handguns deliberately, or negligently, in such a manner that they are at least partially exposed to view. Whether this is a macho thing, or done to intimidate others, or done simply because an individual is stupid, it is unnecessary and inexcusable.

When you talk about concealed carry, the emphasis is on "concealed." Nobody in your presence should know you are carrying a firearm. There are some serious reasons for this, as we alluded to in an earlier chapter.

First, of course, creating a public disturbance by having some alarmed fellow citizen call the police will earn you nothing but trouble, and humiliation.

Second, there is always the potential that you will be caught, by circumstances beyond your control, in the middle of a crime scene, perhaps an armed robbery at a fast food mart, or worse yet, in a bank. If your gun is worn so that someone can spot it, guess who stands the best chance of being shot first if anything goes wrong?

Among my pet peeves are cross-draw holsters worn in such a manner that the butt of the handgun is visibly protruding from behind a jacket or vest.

Another cardinal sin is carrying a gun in a long holster, while wearing a short jacket or vest. This is particularly true if you wear a baseball-type jacket with an elastic waist. These tend to constrict and "ride up" your waist, thus allowing the bottom of a holster to visibly project downward. The worst holster-clothing combinations in this case are nylon holsters and with these jackets, because the elastic waist clings to the nylon holster surface like a magnet.

Paddle holsters can be great offenders, also. While they are designed with the best of intentions, and there are some truly good models out there, you will also find paddle holsters that do not tuck the gun in close to the body, but actually allow the firearm's butt to lean away from the body. This causes the gun to "print" through whatever cover garment you are wearing.

Shoulder holsters are another matter. Straight drop rigs for larger handguns require the body figure to wear them comfortably and naturally, and a long enough garment to cover them. Remember, not everyone has the physical stature of Clint Eastwood, and even if we did, it does take the right camera angle to keep a gun the size of a .44 magnum hidden from view.

Horizontal holsters likewise demand certain wardrobe choices. Remember the "Sonny Crockett" character in "*Miami Vice*" typically wore rather loose, even baggy jackets to adequately hide his large semi auto. Even then, again it takes some camera trickery to make it work, and you're not on television. This is real life.

My suggestion is to carry a smaller pistol if you wear a shoulder rig, and spend the range time necessary to become proficient with that firearm.

Upside-down holsters also require attention to wardrobe, though I've worn one while carrying a Model 19 S&W Combat Magnum under a loose sweatshirt to various sporting events, and nobody was the wiser.

> ***"Nobody in your presence should know you are carrying a firearm."***

What about fanny packs? We mentioned them earlier. Once largely in style, they are not as popular these days, and those who wear ones specifically designed to hold a pistol can generally be recognized by other gunnies, police and bad guys at a glance. There are places that a fanny pack is simply out of place, and you certainly will not wear one to a formal event, or with any kind of business attire.

Be advised that heightened security due to the threat of terrorist incident has police searching backpacks and fanny packs at public events, especially baseball games at Seattle's Safeco Field and Qwest Field.

There are some people who carry guns in their pockets. One guy packs his .38 Special in loose fitting casual pants and nobody knows. Another has his in a pocket holster, again with not much notice. However, I have seen fools carry a gun in the hip pocket of tight jeans, with the grip frame completely visible.

Pancake or belt-slide style holsters are pretty good choices, as they tuck pistols close. They should be worn with shorter-barreled handguns, though, for reasons mentioned above. They can also project below a short jacket or vest.

Be sure if you wear a belt holster, you use a stout enough belt to hold up your gun and trousers. Forget thin dress belts. Buy yourself a good quality dress belt at least one inch wide. If it's two layers of leather stitched together, even better, because these tend to be stiffer. My belts are more than an inch wide, and don't be concerned about such belts not being in fashion. You're not at a fashion show, you're carrying a firearm with which you may have to defend your life.

It comes down to either being practical and staying alive, or being stylish and possibly dead. Your choice.

Chapter Nine
PROTECT YOUR GUN RIGHTS

Your gun rights are important, not only to you, but to other shooters. The licensed, law-abiding citizen who carries concealed has an obligation to follow the law. This obligation is not only to himself, and to the community, but to every other licensed private citizen.

There are several things you, as a gun owner, can do to protect your rights.

•First, seek competent instruction, and learn to be responsible with your firearms.

•Join a gun club. This will open the door not only to recreational shooting opportunities, but many gun clubs either offer, or can refer you to, basic and advanced firearms and personal protection instruction.

•Join the National Rifle Association and the Washington Arms Collectors. This is not the time to wimp out or take issue with the NRA's "radical" political stance. Having served on the NRA's Board of Directors, the author can say with considerable authority that the NRA is not nearly as radical or extreme in its defense of gun rights as, a) NRA's detractors in Congress and the media would have the public believe, and, b) it could, and maybe should, be.

The NRA fights hard to protect the gun rights of honest, law-abiding citizens. It does not, and never has, sought to arm criminals, promoted carrying guns in schools by students, or fought for so-called "cop-killer" armor-piercing bullets.

What NRA has done is fight legislation that was deliberately designed to disarm honest citizens under the guise of crime control; opposed legislation that would restrict right-to-carry by licensed adults under the guise of juvenile crime control; helped defeat legislation that would have made illegal virtually every modern hunting rifle bullet because they have the capability of penetrating some soft body armor.

Membership in the NRA costs $35 a year, and it's the best investment you can make to protect your gun rights.

You should also support both the Second Amendment Foundation (SAF) and the Citizens Committee for the Right to Keep and Bear Arms (CCRKBA). These organizations are based in Bellevue, and have done a tremendous job in educating citizens across the country about their Constitutional rights, and defending those rights in court.

SAF, incidentally, maintains a list of attorneys around the nation who are available to take on firearms rights-related cases.

Now, if you have already bought off on arguments that NRA, SAF or CCRKBA are extremist organizations, and have used this as a reason not to join or support their efforts financially, then you have already lost.

Even worse is the excuse that you have not joined because "I don't want my name on any list." If you have a Social Security number, driver's license, concealed pistol license, hunting license, checking and savings accounts, credit cards and voter registration card, your name is on a list.

•Become politically active in your local party precinct caucuses. When you attend these, and other meetings, dress appropriately. Leave your: a) dirty baseball caps, b) obscene baseball caps, c) slogan T-shirts, d) dirty coveralls, e) camo clothing, etc., at home. Take a bath. Get a haircut. Shave.

•Watch your language and your conduct in public meetings, and do not attend these meetings packing a concealed firearm that will print on your clothing.

•Watch your image. This is extremely important when meeting with elected officials. Several years ago, I attended a hometown meeting with a member of Congress. Another member of my gun club was also there, dressed in dirty denim overalls and rubber boots. He had not shaved for several days, and appeared to have not taken a bath in at least that long. He began complaining loudly and somewhat hysterically, that "I could kill you just as fast with a bolt-action rifle as I could with a semi auto."

If you have people like this in your ranks, discourage them from attending such meetings.

•Make firearms rights your political litmus test for politicians seeking your vote. It is far easier to educate some Neanderthal about important issues such as education, health care and public safety than it is to educate some twit about the importance of protecting your gun rights. Be willing to work with these people, but be careful that you are not blind sided by an anti-gun vote.

•Don't think you can ignore the law and get away with it by claiming a Second Amendment defense.

•Never walk around with a firearm in a deliberately provocative manner. As we discussed in the previous chapter, people who stuff a pistol in their waistband, so that the butt will show if their jacket or vest is open, are not simply stupid or arrogant, they are stupid and arrogant. They will cause trouble not only for themselves, but for every other licensed private citizen. There is a vast difference between having your concealed handgun accidentally show in the event a gust of wind blows your jacket or vest open, and deliberately carrying that gun in such a manner that it "warrants alarm in another person."

•Practice gun safety always. The media loves to publicize gun accidents, and gun control proponents love to use each accident as more proof that further restrictions are necessary.

•Know your elected representatives, from your county council member or commissioner, to your state representative and state senator, and your congressional representative. It is appalling how many gun owners do not know the name of the person who represents them in the legislature or in Congress.

•VOTE! If you do not exercise your right to vote, you are being foolish, and further, you have no right to complain about any legislation that infringes on your firearms rights.

APPENDIX

The following is a roundup of Washington State laws pertaining to concealed carry and the use of force, including lethal force, by private citizens and public officers. Questions about the interpretation of these laws should be addressed to an attorney.

Possession, Purchase

RCW 9.41.040 (2005 c 453 § 1; 2003 c 53 § 26; 1997 c 338 § 47; 1996 c 295 § 2. Prior: 1995 c 129 § 16 (Initiative Measure No. 159); 1994 sp.s. c 7 § 402; prior: 1992 c 205 § 118; 1992 c 168 § 2; 1983 c 232 § 2; 1961 c 124 § 3; 1935 c 172 § 4; RRS § 2516-4.) Unlawful possession of firearms — Ownership, possession by certain persons — Penalties.

(1)(a) A person, whether an adult or juvenile, is guilty of the crime of unlawful possession of a firearm in the first degree, if the person owns, has in his or her possession, or has in his or her control any firearm after having previously been convicted or found not guilty by reason of insanity in this state or elsewhere of any serious offense as defined in this chapter.

(b) Unlawful possession of a firearm in the first degree is a class B felony punishable according to chapter 9A.20 RCW.

(2)(a) A person, whether an adult or juvenile, is guilty of the crime of unlawful possession of a firearm in the second degree, if the person does not qualify under subsection (1) of this section for the crime of unlawful possession of a firearm in the first degree and the person owns, has in his or her possession, or has in his or her control any firearm:

(i) After having previously been convicted or found not guilty by reason of insanity in this state or elsewhere of any felony not specifically listed as prohibiting firearm possession under subsection (1) of this section, or any of the following crimes when committed by one family or household member against another, committed on or after July 1, 1993: Assault in the fourth degree, coercion, stalking, reckless endangerment, criminal trespass in the first degree, or violation of the provisions of a protection order or no-contact order restraining the person or excluding the person from a residence (RCW 26.50.060, 26.50.070, 26.50.130, or 10.99.040);

(ii) After having previously been involuntarily committed for mental health treatment under RCW 71.05.320, 71.34.090, chapter 10.77 RCW, or equivalent statutes of another jurisdiction, unless his or her right to possess a firearm has been restored as provided in RCW 9.41.047;

(iii) If the person is under eighteen years of age, except as provided in RCW 9.41.042; and/or

(iv) If the person is free on bond or personal recognizance pending trial, appeal, or sentencing for a serious offense as defined in RCW 9.41.010.

(b) Unlawful possession of a firearm in the second degree is a class C felony punishable according to chapter 9A.20 RCW.

(3) Notwithstanding RCW 9.41.047 or any other provisions of law, as used in this chapter, a person has been "convicted", whether in an adult court or adjudicated in a juvenile court, at such time as a plea of guilty has been accepted, or a verdict of guilty has been filed, notwithstanding the pendency of any future proceedings including but not limited to sentencing or disposition, post-trial or post-factfinding motions, and appeals. Conviction includes a dismissal entered after a period of probation, suspension or deferral of sentence, and also includes equivalent dispositions by courts in jurisdictions other than Washington state. A person shall

not be precluded from possession of a firearm if the conviction has been the subject of a pardon, annulment, certificate of rehabilitation, or other equivalent procedure based on a finding of the rehabilitation of the person convicted or the conviction or disposition has been the subject of a pardon, annulment, or other equivalent procedure based on a finding of innocence. Where no record of the court's disposition of the charges can be found, there shall be a rebuttable presumption that the person was not convicted of the charge.

(4) Notwithstanding subsection (1) or (2) of this section, a person convicted or found not guilty by reason of insanity of an offense prohibiting the possession of a firearm under this section other than murder, manslaughter, robbery, rape, indecent liberties, arson, assault, kidnapping, extortion, burglary, or violations with respect to controlled substances under RCW 69.50.401 and 69.50.410, who received a probationary sentence under RCW 9.95.200, and who received a dismissal of the charge under RCW 9.95.240, shall not be precluded from possession of a firearm as a result of the conviction or finding of not guilty by reason of insanity. Notwithstanding any other provisions of this section, if a person is prohibited from possession of a firearm under subsection (1) or (2) of this section and has not previously been convicted or found not guilty by reason of insanity of a sex offense prohibiting firearm ownership under subsection (1) or (2) of this section and/or any felony defined under any law as a class A felony or with a maximum sentence of at least twenty years, or both, the individual may petition a court of record to have his or her right to possess a firearm restored:

(a) Under RCW 9.41.047; and/or

(b)(i) If the conviction or finding of not guilty by reason of insanity was for a felony offense, after five or more consecutive years in the community without being convicted or found not guilty by reason of insanity or currently charged with any felony, gross misdemeanor, or misdemeanor crimes, if the individual has no prior felony convictions that prohibit the possession of a firearm counted as part of the offender score under RCW 9.94A.525; or

(ii) If the conviction or finding of not guilty by reason of insanity was for a nonfelony offense, after three or more consecutive years in the community without being convicted or found not guilty by reason of insanity or currently charged with any felony, gross misdemeanor, or misdemeanor crimes, if the individual has no prior felony convictions that prohibit the possession of a firearm counted as part of the offender score under RCW 9.94A.525 and the individual has completed all conditions of the sentence.

(5) In addition to any other penalty provided for by law, if a person under the age of eighteen years is found by a court to have possessed a firearm in a vehicle in violation of subsection (1) or (2) of this section or to have committed an offense while armed with a firearm during which offense a motor vehicle served an integral function, the court shall notify the department of licensing within twenty-four hours and the person's privilege to drive shall be revoked under RCW 46.20.265.

(6) Nothing in chapter 129, Laws of 1995 shall ever be construed or interpreted as preventing an offender from being charged and subsequently convicted for the separate felony crimes of theft of a firearm or possession of a stolen firearm, or both, in addition to being charged and subsequently convicted under this section for unlawful possession of a firearm in the first or second degree. Notwithstanding any other law, if the offender is convicted under this section for unlawful possession of a firearm in the first or second degree and for the felony crimes of theft of a firearm or possession of a stolen firearm, or both, then the offender shall serve consecutive sentences for each of the felony crimes of conviction listed in this subsection.

(7) Each firearm unlawfully possessed under this section shall be a separate offense.

RCW 9.41.042 (2003 c 53 § 27; 1999 c 143 § 2; 1994 sp.s. c 7 § 403.) — Children — Permissible firearm possession.

RCW 9.41.040(2)(a)(iii) shall not apply to any person under the age of eighteen years who is:

(1) In attendance at a hunter's safety course or a firearms safety course;

(2) Engaging in practice in the use of a firearm or target shooting at an established range authorized by the governing body of the jurisdiction in which such range is located or any other area where the discharge of a firearm is not prohibited;

(3) Engaging in an organized competition involving the use of a firearm, or participating in or practicing for a performance by an organized group that uses firearms as a part of the performance;

(4) Hunting or trapping under a valid license issued to the person under Title 77 RCW;

(5) In an area where the discharge of a firearm is permitted, is not trespassing, and the person either: (a) Is at least fourteen years of age, has been issued a hunter safety certificate, and is using a lawful firearm other than a pistol; or (b) is under the supervision of a parent, guardian, or other adult approved for the purpose by the parent or guardian;

(6) Traveling with any unloaded firearm in the person's possession to or from any activity described in subsection (1), (2), (3), (4), or (5) of this section;

(7) On real property under the control of his or her parent, other relative, or legal guardian and who has the permission of the parent or legal guardian to possess a firearm;

(8) At his or her residence and who, with the permission of his or her parent or legal guardian, possesses a firearm for the purpose of exercising the rights specified in RCW 9A.16.020(3); or

(9) Is a member of the armed forces of the United States, national guard, or organized reserves, when on duty.

RCW 9.41.080 (1994 sp.s. c 7 § 409; 1935 c 172 § 8; RRS § 2516-8) Delivery to ineligible persons.

No person may deliver a firearm to any person whom he or she has reasonable cause to believe is ineligible under RCW 9.41.040 to possess a firearm. Any person violating this section is guilty of a class C felony, punishable under chapter 9A.20 RCW.

RCW 9.41.090 (1996 c 295 § 8. Prior: 1994 sp.s. c 7 § 410; 1994 c 264 § 1; 1988 c 36 § 2; 1985 c 428 § 4; 1983 c 232 § 4; 1969 ex.s. c 227 § 1; 1961 c 124 § 7; 1935 c 172 § 9; RRS § 2516-9.) — Dealer deliveries regulated — Hold on delivery.

(1) In addition to the other requirements of this chapter, no dealer may deliver a pistol to the purchaser thereof until:

(a) The purchaser produces a valid concealed pistol license and the dealer has recorded the purchaser's name, license number, and issuing agency, such record to be made in triplicate and processed as provided in subsection (5) of this section. For purposes of this subsection (1)(a), a "valid concealed pistol license" does not include a temporary emergency license, and does not include any license issued before July 1, 1996, unless the issuing agency conducted a records search for disqualifying crimes under RCW 9.41.070 at the time of issuance;

(b) The dealer is notified in writing by the chief of police or the sheriff of the jurisdiction in which the purchaser resides that the purchaser is eligible to possess a pistol under RCW 9.41.040 and that the application to purchase is approved by the chief of police or sheriff; or

(c) Five business days, meaning days on which state offices are open, have elapsed from the time of receipt of the application for the purchase thereof as provided herein by the chief of police or sheriff designated in subsection (5) of this section, and, when delivered, the pistol shall be securely wrapped and shall be unloaded. However, if the purchaser does not have a valid permanent Washington driver's license or state identification card or has not been a resident of the state for the previous consecutive ninety days, the waiting period under this subsection (1)(c) shall be up to sixty days.

(2)(a) Except as provided in (b) of this subsection, in determining whether the purchaser meets the requirements of RCW 9.41.040, the chief of police or sheriff, or the designee of either, shall check with the national crime information center, the Washington state patrol electronic data base, the department of social and health services electronic data base, and with other agencies or resources as appropriate, to determine whether the applicant is ineligible under RCW 9.41.040 to possess a firearm.

(b) Once the system is established, a dealer shall use the state system and national instant criminal background check system, provided for by the Brady Handgun Violence Prevention Act (18 U.S.C. Sec. 921 et seq.), to make criminal background checks of applicants to purchase firearms. However, a chief of police or sheriff, or a designee of either, shall continue to check the department of social and health services' electronic data base and with other agencies or resources as appropriate, to determine whether applicants are ineligible under RCW 9.41.040 to possess a firearm.

(3) In any case under subsection (1)(c) of this section where the applicant has an outstanding warrant for his or her arrest from any court of competent jurisdiction for a felony or misdemeanor, the dealer shall hold the delivery of the pistol until the warrant for arrest is served and satisfied by appropriate court appearance. The local jurisdiction for purposes of the sale shall confirm the existence of outstanding warrants within seventy-two hours after notification of the application to purchase a pistol is received. The local jurisdiction shall also immediately confirm the satisfaction of the warrant on request of the dealer so that the hold may be released if the warrant was for an offense other than an offense making a person ineligible under RCW 9.41.040 to possess a pistol.

(4) In any case where the chief or sheriff of the local jurisdiction has reasonable grounds based on the following circumstances: (a) Open criminal charges, (b) pending criminal proceedings, (c) pending commitment proceedings, (d) an outstanding warrant for an offense making a person ineligible under RCW 9.41.040 to possess a pistol, or (e) an arrest for an offense making a person ineligible under RCW 9.41.040 to possess a pistol, if the records of disposition have not yet been reported or entered sufficiently to determine eligibility to purchase a pistol, the local jurisdiction may hold the sale and delivery of the pistol beyond five days up to thirty days in order to confirm existing records in this state or elsewhere. After thirty days, the hold will be lifted unless an extension of the thirty days is approved by a local district court or municipal court for good cause shown. A dealer shall be notified of each hold placed on the sale by local law enforcement and of any application to the court for additional hold period to confirm records or confirm the identity of the applicant.

(5) At the time of applying for the purchase of a pistol, the purchaser shall sign in triplicate and deliver to the dealer an application containing his or her full name,

residential address, date and place of birth, race, and gender; the date and hour of the application; the applicant's driver's license number or state identification card number; a description of the pistol including the make, model, caliber and manufacturer's number if available at the time of applying for the purchase of a pistol. If the manufacturer's number is not available, the application may be processed, but delivery of the pistol to the purchaser may not occur unless the manufacturer's number is recorded on the application by the dealer and transmitted to the chief of police of the municipality or the sheriff of the county in which the purchaser resides; and a statement that the purchaser is eligible to possess a pistol under RCW 9.41.040.

The application shall contain a warning substantially as follows:

CAUTION: Although state and local laws do not differ, federal law and state law on the possession of firearms differ. If you are prohibited by federal law from possessing a firearm, you may be prosecuted in federal court. State permission to purchase a firearm is not a defense to a federal prosecution.

The purchaser shall be given a copy of the department of fish and wildlife pamphlet on the legal limits of the use of firearms, firearms safety, and the fact that local laws and ordinances on firearms are preempted by state law and must be consistent with state law.

The dealer shall, by the end of the business day, sign and attach his or her address and deliver a copy of the application and such other documentation as required under subsection (1) of this section to the chief of police of the municipality or the sheriff of the county of which the purchaser is a resident. The triplicate shall be retained by the dealer for six years. The dealer shall deliver the pistol to the purchaser following the period of time specified in this section unless the dealer is notified of an investigative hold under subsection (4) of this section in writing by the chief of police of the municipality or the sheriff of the county, whichever is applicable, denying the purchaser's application to purchase and the grounds thereof. The application shall not be denied unless the purchaser is not eligible to possess a pistol under RCW 9.41.040 or 9.41.045, or federal law.

The chief of police of the municipality or the sheriff of the county shall retain or destroy applications to purchase a pistol in accordance with the requirements of 18 U.S.C. Sec. 922.

(6) A person who knowingly makes a false statement regarding identity or eligibility requirements on the application to purchase a pistol is guilty of false swearing under RCW 9A.72.040.

(7) This section does not apply to sales to licensed dealers for resale or to the sale of antique firearms.

RCW 9.41.098 (2003 c 39 § 5; 1996 c 295 § 10; 1994 sp.s. c 7 § 414; 1993 c 243 § 1; 1989 c 222 § 8; 1988 c 223 § 2. Prior: 1987 c 506 § 91; 1987 c 373 § 7; 1986 c 153 § 1; 1983 c 232 § 6.) — Forfeiture of firearms — Disposition — Confiscation.

(1) The superior courts and the courts of limited jurisdiction of the state may order forfeiture of a firearm which is proven to be:

(a) Found concealed on a person not authorized by RCW 9.41.060 or 9.41.070 to carry a concealed pistol: PROVIDED, That it is an absolute defense to forfeiture if the person possessed a valid Washington concealed pistol license within the preceding two years and has not become ineligible for a concealed pistol license in the interim. Before the firearm may be returned, the person must pay the past due renewal fee and the current renewal fee;

(b) Commercially sold to any person without an application as required by RCW 9.41.090;

(c) In the possession of a person prohibited from possessing the firearm under RCW 9.41.040 or 9.41.045;

(d) In the possession or under the control of a person at the time the person committed or was arrested for committing a felony or committing a nonfelony crime in which a firearm was used or displayed;

(e) In the possession of a person who is in any place in which a concealed pistol license is required, and who is under the influence of any drug or under the influence of intoxicating liquor, as defined in chapter 46.61 RCW;

(f) In the possession of a person free on bail or personal recognizance pending trial, appeal, or sentencing for a felony or for a nonfelony crime in which a firearm was used or displayed, except that violations of Title 77 RCW shall not result in forfeiture under this section;

(g) In the possession of a person found to have been mentally incompetent while in possession of a firearm when apprehended or who is thereafter committed pursuant to chapter 10.77 or 71.05 RCW;

(h) Used or displayed by a person in the violation of a proper written order of a court of general jurisdiction; or

(i) Used in the commission of a felony or of a nonfelony crime in which a firearm was used or displayed.

RCW 9.41.240 (1994 sp.s. c 7 § 423; 1971 c 34 § 1; 1909 c 249 § 308; 1883 p 67 § 1;RRS § 2560.) — Possession of pistol by person from eighteen to twenty-one.

Unless an exception under RCW 9.41.042, 9.41.050, or 9.41.060 applies, a person at least eighteen years of age, but less than twenty-one years of age, may possess a pistol only:

(1) In the person's place of abode;

(2) At the person's fixed place of business; or

(3) On real property under his or her control.

RCW 77.15.460 (1999 c 258 § 7; 1998 c 190 § 28.) Loaded firearm in vehicle — Unlawful use or possession — Penalty.

(1) A person is guilty of unlawful possession of a loaded firearm in a motor vehicle if:

(a) The person carries, transports, conveys, possesses, or controls a rifle or shotgun in or on a motor vehicle; and

(b) The rifle or shotgun contains shells or cartridges in the magazine or chamber, or is a muzzle-loading firearm that is loaded and capped or primed.

(2) A person is guilty of unlawful use of a loaded firearm if the person negligently shoots a firearm from, across, or along the maintained portion of a public highway.

(3) Unlawful possession of a loaded firearm in a motor vehicle or unlawful use of a loaded firearm is a misdemeanor.

(4) This section does not apply if the person:

(a) Is a law enforcement officer who is authorized to carry a firearm and is on duty within the officer's respective jurisdiction;

(b) Possesses a disabled hunter's permit as provided by RCW 77.32.237 and complies with all rules of the department concerning hunting by persons with disabilities.

(5) For purposes of this section, a firearm shall not be considered loaded if the detachable clip or magazine is not inserted in or attached to the firearm.

TITLE 18 U.S.C., § 922 (RELEVANT SECTIONS)
Possession of Handgun, Age restriction

(b) It shall be unlawful for any licensed importer, licensed manufacturer, licensed dealer, or licensed collector to sell or deliver

(1) any firearm or ammunition to any individual who the licensee knows or has reasonable cause to believe is less than eighteen years of age, and, if the firearm, or ammunition is other than a shotgun or rifle, or ammunition for a shotgun or rifle, to any individual who the licensee knows or has reasonable cause to believe is less than twenty-one years of age;

Restraining order / Domestic violence

(g) It shall be unlawful for any person-....

(8) who is subject to a court order that-

(A) was issued after a hearing of which such person received actual notice, and at which such person had an opportunity to participate;

(B) restrains such person from harassing, stalking, or threatening an intimate partner of such person or child of such intimate partner or person, or engaging in other conduct that would place an intimate partner in reasonable fear of bodily injury to the partner or child; and

(C)(i) includes a finding that such person represents a credible threat to the physical safety of such intimate partner or child; or

(ii) by its terms explicitly prohibits the use, attempted use, or threatened use of physical force against such intimate partner or child that would reasonably be expected to cause bodily injury; or....

to ship or transport in interstate or foreign commerce, or possess in or affecting commerce, any firearm or ammunition; or to receive any firearm or ammunition which has been shipped or transported in interstate or foreign commerce.

CONCEALED CARRY

RCW 9.41.050 (2003 c 53 § 28; 1997 c 200 § 1; 1996 c 295 § 4; 1994 sp.s. c 7 § 405; 1982 1st ex.s. c 47 § 3; 1961 c 124 § 4; 1935 c 172 § 5; RRS § 2516-5.) — Carrying firearms.

(1)(a) Except in the person's place of abode or fixed place of business, a person shall not carry a pistol concealed on his or her person without a license to carry a concealed pistol.

(b) Every licensee shall have his or her concealed pistol license in his or her immediate possession at all times that he or she is required by this section to have a concealed pistol license and shall display the same upon demand to any police officer or to any other person when and if required by law to do so. Any violation of this subsection (1)(b) shall be a class 1 civil infraction under chapter 7.80 RCW and shall be punished accordingly pursuant to chapter 7.80 RCW and the infraction rules for courts of limited jurisdiction.

(2)(a) A person shall not carry or place a loaded pistol in any vehicle unless the person has a license to carry a concealed pistol and: (i) The pistol is on the licensee's person, (ii) the licensee is within the vehicle at all times that the pistol is there, or (iii) the licensee is away from the vehicle and the pistol is locked within the vehicle and concealed from view from outside the vehicle.

(b) A violation of this subsection is a misdemeanor.

(3)(a) A person at least eighteen years of age who is in possession of an unloaded pistol shall not leave the unloaded pistol in a vehicle unless the unloaded pistol is locked within the vehicle and concealed from view from outside the vehicle.

(b) A violation of this subsection is a misdemeanor.

(4) Nothing in this section permits the possession of firearms illegal to possess under state or federal law.

RCW 9.41.060 (2005 c 453 § 3; 1998 c 253 § 2; 1996 c 295 § 5; 1995 c 392 § 1; 1994 sp.s. c 7 § 406; 1961 c 124 § 5; 1935 c 172 § 6; RRS § 2516-6.) – Exceptions to restrictions on carrying firearms

The provisions of RCW 9.41.050 shall not apply to:

(4) Any person engaged in the business of manufacturing, repairing, or dealing in firearms, or the agent or representative of the person, if possessing, using, or carrying a pistol in the usual or ordinary course of the business;

(5) Regularly enrolled members of any organization duly authorized to purchase or receive pistols from the United States or from this state;

(6) Regularly enrolled members of clubs organized for the purpose of target shooting, when those members are at or are going to or from their places of target practice;

(7) Regularly enrolled members of clubs organized for the purpose of modern and antique firearm collecting, when those members are at or are going to or from their collector's gun shows and exhibits;

(8) Any person engaging in a lawful outdoor recreational activity such as hunting, fishing, camping, hiking, or horseback riding, only if, considering all of the attendant circumstances, including but not limited to whether the person has a valid hunting or fishing license, it is reasonable to conclude that the person is participating in lawful outdoor activities or is traveling to or from a legitimate outdoor recreation area;

(9) Any person while carrying a pistol unloaded and in a closed opaque case or secure wrapper…

RCW 9.41.070 (2002 c 302 § 703; 1999 c 222 § 2; 1996 c 295 § 6; 1995 c 351 § 1. Prior: 1994 sp.s. c 7 § 407; 1994 c 190 § 2; 1992 c 168 § 1; 1990 c 195 § 6; prior: 1988 c 263 § 10; 1988 c 223 § 1; 1988 c 219 § 1; 1988 c 36 § 1; 1985 c 428 § 3; 1983 c 232 § 3; 1979 c 158 § 1; 1971 ex.s. c 302 § 2; 1961 c 124 § 6; 1935 c 172 § 7; RRS § 2516-7.) — Concealed pistol license — Application — Fee — Renewal.

(1) The chief of police of a municipality or the sheriff of a county shall within thirty days after the filing of an application of any person, issue a license to such person to carry a pistol concealed on his or her person within this state for five years from date of issue, for the purposes of protection or while engaged in business, sport, or while traveling. However, if the applicant does not have a valid permanent Washington driver's license or Washington state identification card or has not been a resident of the state for the previous consecutive ninety days, the issuing authority shall have up to sixty days after the filing of the application to issue a license. The issuing authority shall not refuse to accept completed applications for concealed pistol licenses during regular business hours.

The applicant's constitutional right to bear arms shall not be denied, unless:

(a) He or she is ineligible to possess a firearm under the provisions of RCW 9.41.040 or 9.41.045;

(b) The applicant's concealed pistol license is in a revoked status;

(c) He or she is under twenty-one years of age;

(d) He or she is subject to a court order or injunction regarding firearms pursuant to RCW 9A.46.080, 10.14.080, 10.99.040, 10.99.045, 26.09.050, 26.09.060,

26.10.040, 26.10.115, 26.26.130, 26.50.060, 26.50.070, or 26.26.590;

(e) He or she is free on bond or personal recognizance pending trial, appeal, or sentencing for a felony offense;

(f) He or she has an outstanding warrant for his or her arrest from any court of competent jurisdiction for a felony or misdemeanor; or

(g) He or she has been ordered to forfeit a firearm under RCW 9.41.098(1)(e) within one year before filing an application to carry a pistol concealed on his or her person.

No person convicted of a felony may have his or her right to possess firearms restored or his or her privilege to carry a concealed pistol restored, unless the person has been granted relief from disabilities by the secretary of the treasury under 18 U.S.C. Sec. 925(c), or RCW 9.41.040 (3) or (4) applies.

(2) The issuing authority shall check with the national crime information center, the Washington state patrol electronic data base, the department of social and health services electronic data base, and with other agencies or resources as appropriate, to determine whether the applicant is ineligible under RCW 9.41.040 or 9.41.045 to possess a firearm and therefore ineligible for a concealed pistol license. This subsection applies whether the applicant is applying for a new concealed pistol license or to renew a concealed pistol license.

(3) Any person whose firearms rights have been restricted and who has been granted relief from disabilities by the secretary of the treasury under 18 U.S.C. Sec. 925(c) or who is exempt under 18 U.S.C. Sec. 921(a)(20)(A) shall have his or her right to acquire, receive, transfer, ship, transport, carry, and possess firearms in accordance with Washington state law restored except as otherwise prohibited by this chapter....

(13) A person may apply for a concealed pistol license:

(a) To the municipality or to the county in which the applicant resides if the applicant resides in a municipality;

(b) To the county in which the applicant resides if the applicant resides in an unincorporated area; or

(c) Anywhere in the state if the applicant is a nonresident.

RCW 9.41.073 (2004 c 148 § 1.) Concealed pistol license—Reciprocity.

(1)(a) A person licensed to carry a pistol in a state the laws of which recognize and give effect in that state to a concealed pistol license issued under the laws of the state of Washington is authorized to carry a concealed pistol in this state if:

(i) The licensing state does not issue concealed pistol licenses to persons under twenty-one years of age; and

(ii) The licensing state requires mandatory fingerprint-based background checks of criminal and mental health history for all persons who apply for a concealed pistol license.

(b) This section applies to a license holder from another state only while the license holder is not a resident of this state. A license holder from another state must carry the handgun in compliance with the laws of this state.

(2) The attorney general shall periodically publish a list of states the laws of which recognize and give effect in that state to a concealed pistol license issued under the laws of the state of Washington and which meet the requirements of subsection (1)(a)(i) and (ii) of this section.

RCW 9.41.075 (2005 c 453 § 4; 1994 sp.s. c 7 § 408) – Concealed pistol license – Revocation.

(1) The license shall be revoked by the license-issuing authority immediately upon:

(a) Discovery by the issuing authority that the person was ineligible under RCW 9.41.070 for a concealed pistol license when applying for the license or license renewal;

(b) Conviction of the licensee, or the licensee being found not guilty by reason of insanity, of an offense, or commitment of the licensee for mental health treatment, that makes a person ineligible under RCW 9.41.040 to possess a firearm;

(c) Conviction of the licensee for a third violation of this chapter within five calendar years; or

(d) An order that the licensee forfeit a firearm under RCW 9.41.098(1)(d).

(2)(a) Unless the person may lawfully possess a pistol without a concealed pistol license, an ineligible person to whom a concealed pistol license was issued shall, within fourteen days of license revocation, lawfully transfer ownership of any pistol acquired while the person was in possession of the license.

(b) Upon discovering a person issued a concealed pistol license was ineligible for the license, the issuing authority shall contact the department of licensing to determine whether the person purchased a pistol while in possession of the license. If the person did purchase a pistol while in possession of the concealed pistol license, if the person may not lawfully possess a pistol without a concealed pistol license, the issuing authority shall require the person to present satisfactory evidence of having lawfully transferred ownership of the pistol. The issuing authority shall require the person to produce the evidence within fifteen days of the revocation of the license.

(3) When a licensee is ordered to forfeit a firearm under RCW 9.41.098(1)(d), the issuing authority shall:

(a) On the first forfeiture, revoke the license for one year;

(b) On the second forfeiture, revoke the license for two years; or

(c) On the third or subsequent forfeiture, revoke the license for five years.

Any person whose license is revoked as a result of a forfeiture of a firearm under RCW 9.41.098(1)(d) may not reapply for a new license until the end of the revocation period.

(4) The issuing authority shall notify, in writing, the department of licensing of the revocation of a license. The department of licensing shall record the revocation.

RCW 9.41.270 (1994 sp.s. c 7 § 426; 1969 c 8 § 1.) Weapons apparently capable of producing bodily harm -Unlawful carrying or handling — Penalty — Exceptions.

(1) It shall be unlawful for any person to carry, exhibit, display, or draw any firearm, dagger, sword, knife or other cutting or stabbing instrument, club, or any other weapon apparently capable of producing bodily harm, in a manner, under circumstances, and at a time and place that either manifests an intent to intimidate another or that warrants alarm for the safety of other persons.

(2) Any person violating the provisions of subsection (1) above shall be guilty of a gross misdemeanor. If any person is convicted of a violation of subsection (1) of this section, the person shall lose his or her concealed pistol license, if any. The court shall send notice of the revocation to the department of licensing, and the city, town, or county which issued the license.

(3) Subsection (1) of this section shall not apply to or affect the following:

(a) Any act committed by a person while in his or her place of abode or fixed place of business;

(b) Any person who by virtue of his or her office or public employment is vested by law with a duty to preserve public safety, maintain public order, or to make arrests for offenses, while in the performance of such duty;

(c) Any person acting for the purpose of protecting himself or herself against the use of presently threatened unlawful force by another, or for the purpose of protecting another against the use of such unlawful force by a third person;

(d) Any person making or assisting in making a lawful arrest for the commission of a felony; or

(e) Any person engaged in military activities sponsored by the federal or state governments.

RCW 9.41.280 (1999 c 167 § 1; 1996 c 295 § 13; 1995 c 87 § 1; 1994 sp.s. c 7 § 427; 1993 c 347 § 1; 1989 c 219 § 1; 1982 1st ex.s. c 47 § 4.) —Possessing dangerous weapons on school facilities — Penalty — Exceptions.

(1) It is unlawful for a person to carry onto, or to possess on, public or private elementary or secondary school premises, school-provided transportation, or areas of facilities while being used exclusively by public or private schools:

(a) Any firearm;

(b) Any other dangerous weapon as defined in RCW 9.41.250;

(c) Any device commonly known as "nun-chu-ka sticks", consisting of two or more lengths of wood, metal, plastic, or similar substance connected with wire, rope, or other means;

(d) Any device, commonly known as "throwing stars", which are multi-pointed, metal objects designed to embed upon impact from any aspect; or

(e) Any air gun, including any air pistol or air rifle, designed to propel a BB, pellet, or other projectile by the discharge of compressed air, carbon dioxide, or other gas.

(2) Any such person violating subsection (1) of this section is guilty of a gross misdemeanor. If any person is convicted of a violation of subsection (1)(a) of this section, the person shall have his or her concealed pistol license, if any revoked for a period of three years. Anyone convicted under this subsection is prohibited from applying for a concealed pistol license for a period of three years. The court shall send notice of the revocation to the department of licensing, and the city, town, or county which issued the license.

Any violation of subsection (1) of this section by elementary or secondary school students constitutes grounds for expulsion from the state's public schools in accordance with RCW 28A.600.010. An appropriate school authority shall promptly notify law enforcement and the student's parent or guardian regarding any allegation or indication of such violation.

Upon the arrest of a person at least twelve years of age and not more than twenty-one years of age for violating subsection (1)(a) of this section, the person shall be detained or confined in a juvenile or adult facility for up to seventy-two hours. The person shall not be released within the seventy-two hours until after the person has been examined and evaluated by the county-designated mental health professional unless the court in its discretion releases the person sooner after a determination regarding probable cause or on probation bond or bail.

Within twenty-four hours of the arrest, the arresting law enforcement agency shall refer the person to the county-designated mental health professional for examination and evaluation under chapter 71.05 or 71.34 RCW and inform a parent or guardian of the person of the arrest, detention, and examination. The county-designated mental health professional shall examine and evaluate the person subject to the provisions of chapter 71.05 or 71.34 RCW. The examination shall occur at the facility in which the person is detained or confined. If the person has been released on probation, bond, or bail, the examination shall occur wherever is appropriate.

The county-designated mental health professional may determine whether to refer the person to the county-designated chemical dependency specialist for examination and evaluation in accordance with chapter 70.96A RCW. The county-designated chemical dependency specialist shall examine the person subject to the provisions of chapter 70.96A RCW. The examination shall occur at the facility in which the person is detained or confined. If the person has been released on probation, bond, or bail, the examination shall occur wherever is appropriate.

Upon completion of any examination by the county-designated mental health professional or the county-designated chemical dependency specialist, the results of the examination shall be sent to the court, and the court shall consider those results in making any determination about the person.

The county-designated mental health professional and county-designated chemical dependency specialist shall, to the extent permitted by law, notify a parent or guardian of the person that an examination and evaluation has taken place and the results of the examination. Nothing in this subsection prohibits the delivery of additional, appropriate mental health examinations to the person while the person is detained or confined.

If the county-designated mental health professional determines it is appropriate, the county-designated mental health professional may refer the person to the local regional support network for follow-up services or the department of social and health services or other community providers for other services to the family and individual.

(3) Subsection (1) of this section does not apply to:

(a) Any student or employee of a private military academy when on the property of the academy;

(b) Any person engaged in military, law enforcement, or school district security activities;

(c) Any person who is involved in a convention, showing, demonstration, lecture, or firearms safety course authorized by school authorities in which the firearms of collectors or instructors are handled or displayed;

(d) Any person while the person is participating in a firearms or air gun competition approved by the school or school district;

(e) Any person in possession of a pistol who has been issued a license under RCW 9.41.070, or is exempt from the licensing requirement by RCW 9.41.060, while picking up or dropping off a student;

(f) Any nonstudent at least eighteen years of age legally in possession of a firearm or dangerous weapon that is secured within an attended vehicle or concealed from view within a locked unattended vehicle while conducting legitimate business at the school;

(g) Any nonstudent at least eighteen years of age who is in lawful possession of an unloaded firearm, secured in a vehicle while conducting legitimate business at the school; or

(h) Any law enforcement officer of the federal, state, or local government agency.

(4) Subsections (1)(c) and (d) of this section do not apply to any person who possesses nun-chu-ka sticks, throwing stars, or other dangerous weapons to be used in martial arts classes authorized to be conducted on the school premises.

(5) Except as provided in subsection (3)(b), (c), (f), and (h) of this section, firearms are not permitted in a public or private school building.

(6) "GUN-FREE ZONE" signs shall be posted around school facilities giving warning of the prohibition of the possession of firearms on school grounds.

RCW 9.41.290 (1994 sp.s. c 7 § 428; 1985 c 428 § 1; 1983 c 232 § 12.) State preemption.

The state of Washington hereby fully occupies and preempts the entire field of firearms regulation within the boundaries of the state, including the registration, licensing, possession, purchase, sale, acquisition, transfer, discharge, and transportation of firearms, or any other element relating to firearms or parts thereof, including ammunition and reloader components. Cities, towns, and counties or other municipalities may enact only those laws and ordinances relating to firearms that are specifically authorized by state law, as in RCW 9.41.300, and are consistent with this chapter. Such local ordinances shall have the same penalty as provided for by state law. Local laws and ordinances that are inconsistent with, more restrictive than, or exceed the requirements of state law shall not be enacted and are preempted and repealed, regardless of the nature of the code, charter, or home rule status of such city, town, county, or municipality.

RCW 9.41.300 (2004 c 116 § 1; 2004 c 16 § 1; 1994 sp.s. c 7 § 429; 1993 c 396 § 1; 1985 c 428 § 2.) — Weapons prohibited in certain places — Local laws and ordinances — Exceptions — Penalty.

(1) It is unlawful for any person to enter the following places when he or she knowingly possesses or knowingly has under his or her control a weapon:

(a) The restricted access areas of a jail, or of a law enforcement facility, or any place used for the confinement of a person (i) arrested for, charged with, or convicted of an offense, (ii) held for extradition or as a material witness, or (iii) otherwise confined pursuant to an order of a court, except an order under chapter 13.32A or 13.34 RCW. Restricted access areas do not include common areas of egress or ingress open to the general public;

(b) Those areas in any building which are used in connection with court proceedings, including courtrooms, jury rooms, judge's chambers, offices and areas used to conduct court business, waiting areas, and corridors adjacent to areas used in connection with court proceedings. The restricted areas do not include common areas of ingress and egress to the building that is used in connection with court proceedings, when it is possible to protect court areas without restricting ingress and egress to the building. The restricted areas shall be the minimum necessary to fulfill the objective of this subsection (1)(b).

In addition, the local legislative authority shall provide either a stationary locked box sufficient in size for pistols and key to a weapon owner for weapon storage, or shall designate an official to receive weapons for safekeeping, during the owner's visit to restricted areas of the building. The locked box or designated official shall be located within the same building used in connection with court proceedings. The local legislative authority shall be liable for any negligence causing damage to or loss of a weapon either placed in a locked box or left with an official during the owner's visit to restricted areas of the building.

The local judicial authority shall designate and clearly mark those areas where weapons are prohibited, and shall post notices at each entrance to the building of the prohibition against weapons in the restricted areas;

(c) The restricted access areas of a public mental health facility certified by the department of social and health services for inpatient hospital care and state institutions for the care of the mentally ill, excluding those facilities solely for evaluation and treatment. Restricted access areas do not include common areas of egress and ingress open to the general public;

(d) That portion of an establishment classified by the state liquor control board as off-limits to persons under twenty-one years of age; or

(e) The restricted access areas of a commercial service airport designated in the airport security plan approved by the federal transportation security administration, including passenger screening checkpoints at or beyond the point at which a passenger initiates the screening process. These areas do not include airport drives, general parking areas and walkways, and shops and areas of the terminal that are outside the screening checkpoints and that are normally open to unscreened passengers or visitors to the airport. Any restricted access area shall be clearly indicated by prominent signs indicating that firearms and other weapons are prohibited in the area.

(2) Cities, towns, counties, and other municipalities may enact laws and ordinances:

(a) Restricting the discharge of firearms in any portion of their respective jurisdictions where there is a reasonable likelihood that humans, domestic animals, or property will be jeopardized. Such laws and ordinances shall not abridge the right of the individual guaranteed by Article I, section 24 of the state Constitution to bear arms in defense of self or others; and

(b) Restricting the possession of firearms in any stadium or convention center, operated by a city, town, county, or other municipality, except that such restrictions shall not apply to:

(i) Any pistol in the possession of a person licensed under RCW 9.41.070 or exempt from the licensing requirement by RCW 9.41.060; or

(ii) Any showing, demonstration, or lecture involving the exhibition of firearms....

(6) Subsection (1) of this section does not apply to:

(b) Law enforcement personnel, except that subsection (1)(b) of this section does apply to a law enforcement officer who is present at a courthouse building as a party to an action under chapter 10.14, 10.99, or 26.50 RCW, or an action under Title 26 RCW where any party has alleged the existence of domestic violence as defined in RCW 26.50.010; or

(7) Subsection (1)(a) of this section does not apply to a person licensed pursuant to RCW 9.41.070 who, upon entering the place or facility, directly and promptly proceeds to the administrator of the facility or the administrator's designee and obtains written permission to possess the firearm while on the premises or checks his or her firearm. The person may reclaim the firearms upon leaving but must immediately and directly depart from the place or facility.

RCW 70.108.150 (1972 ex.s. c 123 § 5) Firearms —Penalty. It shall be unlawful for any person, except law enforcement officers, to carry, transport or convey, or to have in his possession or under his control any firearm while on the site of an outdoor music festival.

Any person violating the provisions of this section shall be guilty of a misdemeanor and upon conviction thereof shall be punished by a fine of not less than one hundred dollars and not more than two hundred dollars or by imprisonment in the county jail for not less than ten days and nor more than ninety days or by both such fine and imprisonment.

RCW 9.91.025 (2004 c 118 § 1; 1994 c 45 § 4; 1992 c 77 § 1; 1984 c 167 § 1.) — Unlawful bus conduct.

(1) A person is guilty of unlawful bus conduct if while on or in a municipal transit vehicle as defined by RCW 46.04.355 or in or at a municipal transit station and with knowledge that the conduct is prohibited, he or she:

(e) Carries any flammable liquid, explosive, acid, or other article or material likely to cause harm to others except that nothing herein prevents a person from carrying a cigarette, cigar, or pipe lighter or carrying a firearm or ammunition in a way that is not otherwise prohibited by law;

COLLEGE CAMPUSES

University of Washington*

WAC 478-124-020 Conduct on campus code — Prohibited conduct. (2) In order to assure those rights to all members of the university community and to maintain a peaceful atmosphere in which the university may continue to make its special contribution to society, the following types of conduct are hereby prohibited on or in property either owned, controlled or operated by the university which is used or set aside for university purposes, hereinafter referred to as the university campus:

(e) Possession or use of firearms, explosives, dangerous chemicals or other dangerous weapons or instrumentalities on the university campus, except for authorized university purposes, unless prior written approval has been obtained from the vice president for student affairs, or any other person designated by the president of the university;

(* Note: This WAC also applies to Harborview Medical Center in Seattle, because it is administered by the University of Washington.)

Washington State University

WAC 504-36-030 Spectator events — Safety rules. (1) Protection of the safety and general welfare of students, faculty and staff, performers and officials, and members of the general public attending or participating in spectator events on the campus is a primary concern of Washington State University.

(2) The following rules of conduct are applicable to all public events of Washington State University, including specifically, but not limited to, Martin Stadium and the Performing Arts Coliseum and to all public areas of the facility wherein the event is held (hereafter the "event site").

(f) Possession of any fireworks, weapons, explosive devices or artificial noisemaking devices (such as air horns) is prohibited in the event site. Any such items shall be surrendered to designated university officials upon request. In addition, possession of such items may subject violators of this rule to university disciplinary action (if applicable) and/or legal proceedings, and to removal from the event site.

Central Washington University

WAC 106-124-700 Firearms, explosives, dangerous chemicals — Restrictions. No person shall have in his possession any gun, pistol, firearm, explosive, dangerous chemicals, or other dangerous weapons or instruments on university-owned or university-leased property except as follows:

(1) Authorized law enforcement officers shall be permitted to carry arms while on duty and engaged in their regular duties;

(2) Activities requiring use of the prohibited items may be conducted upon approval of the president or his designee;

(3) Persons with firearms in their possession shall be permitted to travel enroute to or from the university-provided firearm storage facilities only. Violators of this WAC shall be subject to appropriate disciplinary or legal action.

Eastern Washington University

WAC 172-122-120 Firearms/weapons. Violations of the subsections of this section are subject to appropriate disciplinary or legal action.

(1) Possession, carrying, or discharge of any explosive, firearm, chemical weapon (or dangerous chemical) or other weapon; including shotguns, pistols, air guns, pellet guns, and paint ball guns, whether loaded or unloaded; is prohibited on property owned or controlled by Eastern Washington University.

(2) Only people who are authorized to carry firearms or other weapons as duly appointed and commissioned law enforcement officers in the state of Washington, or commissioned by agencies of the United States government, shall possess firearms or other weapons issued for their possession by their respective law enforcement agencies while on campus or other university-controlled property, including residence halls. A law enforcement agent must notify the university police of his or her presence on campus on arrival.

(3) Other than the people referenced in subsection (2) of this section, members of the campus community and visitors who bring firearms or other weapons to campus must immediately place the firearms or weapons in the university-provided storage facility, located at the red barn. The storage facility is controlled by the university police office and is accessible twenty-four hours per day throughout the year.

(4) Anyone seeking to bring a firearm or other weapon onto campus for display or demonstration purposes directly related to a class or other educational activity must obtain prior authorization from the university police department. The university police department shall review any such request and may establish conditions to the authorization.

(5) Firearms owned by the institution for use by special interest groups such as university-sponsored gun clubs, ROTC, or intercollegiate shooting teams, must be stored in a location approved by the university police department. These firearms must be checked out by the club advisor or coach and are to be used by legitimate members of the club or team in the normal course of the club or team's related activity.

WAC 172-120-040 Conduct code. The following are defined as offenses which are subject to disciplinary action by the university. The university has the authority to promulgate additional or more specific rules supplementary to the offenses listed in this section.

(9) Possession of weapons. No individual shall have on his/her person, in his/her vehicle or otherwise in his/her possession any gun, pistol, or firearm or explosives, dangerous chemicals or other dangerous weapons or instruments on the university campus or other university property except as follows:

(a) Authorized law enforcement officers are permitted to carry arms while on duty and engaged in their regular duties.

(b) Activities requiring use of the prohibited items may be conducted on approval of the activity by the board of trustees.

(c) Persons are permitted to have firearms in their possession directly en route to or from campus firearm storage facilities where such possession is incidental to approved on or off campus possession or use of such firearms.

Western Washington University

WAC 516-52-020 Firearms and dangerous weapons. (1) Only such persons who are authorized to carry firearms or other weapons as duly appointed and commissioned law enforcement officers in the state of Washington, commissioned by agencies of the United States government, or authorized by contract with the university, shall possess firearms or other weapons issued for their possession by their respective law enforcement agencies or employers while on the campus or other university-controlled property, including, but not limited to, residence halls. No one may possess explosives unless licensed to do so for purposes of conducting university-authorized activities relating to building construction or demolition.

(2) Other than the law enforcement officers or other individuals referenced in subsection (1) of this section, members of the campus community and visitors who bring firearms or other weapons to campus must immediately place the firearms or weapons in the university-provided storage facility. The storage facility is located at the university public safety department and is accessible twenty-four hours per day.

(3) If any member of the campus community or visitor wishes to bring a weapon to the campus for display or demonstration purposes directly related to a class, seminar, or other educational activity, permission for such possession may be applied for at the university public safety department, which shall review any such proposal and may establish the conditions of the possession on campus.

Big Bend Community College

WAC 132R-117-010 Firearms and dangerous weapons. (1) Possession, carrying or discharge of any explosive, firearm, or other weapon (including shot guns, pistols, air guns, pellet-guns, and paint-ball guns), whether loaded or unloaded, is prohibited on Big Bend Community College owned or controlled property.

(2) Only such persons who are authorized to carry firearms or other weapons as duly appointed and commissioned law enforcement officers in the state of Washington, and persons or entities authorized by contract to carry firearms in the course of their employment, shall possess firearms or other weapons issued for their possession by their respective law enforcement agencies while on campus or other college controlled property, including residence halls.

(3) Other than the persons referenced in subsection (2) of this section, members of the campus community and visitors who bring firearms or other weapons to campus must immediately place the firearms or weapons in the college-provided storage facility. The storage facility is controlled by the office of student life and is accessible during the hours of 8:00 a.m. through 4:30 p.m., Monday through Friday (excluding holidays).

(4) Anyone seeking to bring a firearm or other weapon onto campus for display or demonstration purposes directly related to a class or other educational activity must obtain prior written authorization from the vice-president of educational services or any other person designated by the president of the college. The vice-president of educational services or other designee shall review any such request and may establish conditions to the authorization.

(5) Firearms owned by the institution for use by special interest groups such as ASB gun clubs, ROTC, or intercollegiate shooting teams, must be stored in a location approved by the dean of student services or any other person designated by the president of the college. Said firearms must be checked out by the club advisor or coach and are to be used by legitimate members of the club or teams in the normal course of the club or team's activity.

(6) Violators shall be subject to appropriate disciplinary or legal action.

Peninsula Community College

WAC 132A-150-020 Firearms, explosives, and dangerous chemicals restrictions. No person shall have in his or her possession on college owned or leased property any guns (including shotguns, rifles, pistols, air guns and pellet guns), firearms, explosives, dangerous chemicals, or other dangerous weapons or instruments. Violation is grounds for disciplinary and/or legal action. Excepted are as follows:

(1) Authorized law enforcement officers carrying guns while engaged in regular duties;

(2) Activities requiring the use of prohibited items, subject to the president's approval.

Everett Community College

WAC 132E-120-220 Student conduct code — Violations. (3) Disciplinary actions and/or sanctions may be imposed on a student for the commission of any of the following offenses:

(p) Failure to comply with the following rules governing firearms and weapons on campus:

(i) Carrying, exhibiting, displaying, or drawing any weapon, such as a slung shot, sand club, metal knuckles, dagger, sword, or swing blade knife, or any knife of which is automatically released by a spring mechanism or other mechanical devise, or any knife having a blade which opens, or falls, or is ejected into position by force of gravity, or by outward, downward, or centrifugal thrust or movement, or any other cutting or stabbing instrument or club or any other weapon apparently capable of inflicting bodily harm and/or property damage is prohibited.

(ii) Explosives, incendiary devices, or any weapon facsimile are prohibited in or on college facilities.

(iii) Carrying firearms on college facilities is prohibited except and unless the firearm is registered with campus safety and security for a designated period of time that the firearm is carried on campus.

(iv) The regulations in (p)(i) through (iii) of this subsection shall not apply to equipment or material owned, used or maintained by the college: Nor will they apply to law enforcement officers.

Highline Community College

WAC 132I-120-100 Student responsibilities. (3) As members of the Highline community, students are expected to obey all college rules and regulations and are prohibited from engaging in any unlawful conduct. Any student shall be subject to disciplinary action as provided for in this chapter (see WAC 132I-120-410)

(d) Failure to comply with the following regulations governing firearms and weapons:

(i) It shall be the policy of the college that carrying, exhibiting, displaying, or drawing any weapon, such as a dagger, sword, knife, or any other cutting or stabbing instrument or club or any other weapons apparently capable of producing bodily harm and/or property damage is prohibited on or in college facilities.

(ii) Explosives, incendiary devices, or any weapon facsimile are prohibited on or in college facilities.

(iii) It shall be the policy of the college that carrying of firearms on college facilities is prohibited except and unless the firearm is registered with the campus security for a specific period of time that the firearm is carried on campus.

(iv) The above regulations shall not apply to equipment or material owned, used, or maintained, by the college; nor will they apply to law enforcement officers.

Seattle Community College

WAC 132F-120-110 Misconduct. The Seattle Community College District defines
misconduct as that which adversely affects the institution's pursuit of its educational objectives.
Irresponsible behavior for which the campuses may impose sanctions is defined as follows:

(10) Possession of firearms, even if licensed to do so except commissioned police officers as prescribed by law.

WAC 132F-136-030 Limitation of use. (9) No person or group may use or enter onto college facilities having in their possession firearms, even if licensed to do so, except commissioned police officers as prescribed by law.

Skagit Valley Community College

WAC 132D-140-040 General policies limiting use. (8) No person or group may use or enter onto college facilities having in their possession firearms, even if licensed to do so, except commissioned police officers as prescribed by law.

Columbia Basin Community College

WAC 132S-50-280 Regulations governing firearms and weapons on or in college facilities. (1) It shall be the policy of this college that possession of weapons apparently capable of producing bodily harm and/or property damage is prohibited on or in college facilities or college-leased facilities.

(2) Explosives are prohibited on or in college facilities or leased college facilities.

(3) Carrying of firearms on or in college facilities or college-leased facilities is prohibited except and unless the firearm is registered with the campus security department for a specified period of time.

(4) The aforementioned regulations shall not apply to equipment or materials owned, used or maintained by the college; nor will they apply to law enforcement officers.

(5) Violations of these rules may be grounds for immediate suspension pending a hearing in accordance with WAC 132S-40-075

Green River Community College

WAC 132J-125-150 Firearms/explosives. Any student who, while in any college facility or participating in a college-related program, uses or has on his/her person firearms or explosive materials, without written permission of the vice-president for marketing and student development or vice-president's designee, shall be subject to discipline.

WAC 132J-141-010 Prohibited activities. It shall be prohibited on or in property either owned, controlled or operated by Green River Community College, District No. 10, for anyone to use or have on his/her person firearms or solid explosives, except duly commissioned law enforcement officers and other individuals who receive written prior approval from the president of the college or his designee. Sanctions for violations of this rule may include, but are not limited to, suspension, dismissal and/or expulsion or removal from campus.

Pierce College

WAC 132K-125-170 Rules and regulations. Any student may be subject to disciplinary action as described in this chapter if the student, whether as a principle actor, aider, abettor or accomplice as defined in RCW 9A.08.020 as now law or hereafter
amended, interferes with the personal rights or privileges of others or with the college's educational process and violates any provision of this chapter. Grounds for disciplinary action include, but are not limited to, the following:

(19) Possession or use (to include exhibiting, displaying or drawing any weapon) of firearms, explosives, other weapons or instrumentalities or dangerous chemicals or any other device or substance which can be used to inflict bodily harm or damage real or personal property on college facilities, except for authorized college purposes or for law enforcement officers.

Centralia Community College

WAC 132L-120-080 Student responsibilities. (5) Students are expected to obey all college rules and regulations and obey the law. Any student shall be subject to disciplinary action as provided for in this code who, either as a principal actor, aider, abettor, or accomplice violates any local, state, or federal law, interferes with the personal rights or privileges of others or the educational process of the college; violates any provision of this code; or commits any of the following prohibited actions. The standard of conduct as listed below should be interpreted by students as general notice of prohibited conduct. They should be read broadly, and are not designed to define misconduct in exhaustive terms:

(mm) Failure to comply with the following regulations governing firearms and weapons:

(i) It shall be the policy of the college that carrying, exhibiting, displaying, or drawing any weapon or weapon facsimile, such as a gun or firearm, dagger, sword, knife, or any other cutting or stabbing instrument or club or any other weapons apparently capable of producing bodily harm and/or property damage is prohibited, in a manner, under circumstances, and at a time and place that either manifests an intent to intimidate another or that warrants alarm for safety of other persons is prohibited.

(ii) Explosives, incendiary devices, or any similar device, object, or product is prohibited.

(iii) The above regulations shall not apply to equipment or material owned, used, or maintained by the college; nor will they apply to law enforcement officers.

Lower Columbia Community College

WAC 132M-136-060 Use of college facilities. (10) No person or group may use or enter college facilities having in their possession firearms or other weapons, even if licensed to do so, except duly appointed and commissioned law enforcement officers.

Yakima Valley Community College

WAC 132P-33-170 Violations. Any student shall be subject to immediate disciplinary action provided for in code procedures and summary suspension rules who, either as a principal actor or aider or abettor:

(3) Commits any of the following acts which are hereby prohibited:

(g) Possession or use of firearms, explosives, dangerous chemicals or other dangerous weapons or instrumentalities on the college campus, except for authorized college purposes; unless prior written approval has been obtained from the dean of students, or any other person designated by the campus president.

Spokane Community College

WAC 132Q-94-150 Prohibition of firearms and other dangerous instrumentalities. No employee, student or guest shall carry, transport within a vehicle or otherwise possess any gun, pistol or other firearm or explosive device, hazardous chemicals or any other hazardous device such as knives or substance on any college campus or other district property except for use in an authorized college activity with express authorization from the chief executive of the campus or an authorized designee.

WAC 132Q-04-031 Prohibited conduct. Disciplinary action may be taken for a violation of any provision of this student code or for a violation of other district and college rules, policies and regulations by a student which may from time to time be properly enacted including, but not limited to, the following:

(16) Possessing, transporting, or storing of any firearm(s), explosives, dangerous chemicals or other weapons, including knives, devices or substances which can be used to inflict bodily harm or to damage real or personal property. This does not apply to commissioned police officers as prescribed by law.

Walla Walla Community College

WAC 132T-190-030 Limitation of use.

(10) No person or group may use or enter onto college facilities having in their possession firearms, even though licensed to do so, except commissioned police officers as prescribed by law.

Whatcom Community College

WAC 132U-140-040 General policies limiting use. (9) No person or group may use or enter onto college facilities having in their possession firearms, even if licensed to do so, except commissioned police officers as prescribed by law.

Tacoma Community College

WAC 132V-120-050 Student responsibilities. Any student who violates any provision of this chapter or who as a principal aids, abets, encourages, or procures another person to materially and substantially interfere with the personal rights or privileges of others or the educational process of the college shall be subject to disciplinary action as provided in this chapter.

Grounds for disciplinary action include the following:

(19) Possession or use of firearms, explosives, dangerous chemicals or other dangerous weapons or instrumentalities.

Wenatchee Valley Community College

WAC 132W-115-080 Code of conduct. Wenatchee Valley College expects that its students while within college facilities or attending a college-sponsored activity, will adhere to high standards of honor and good citizenship at all times. Students will always conduct themselves in a responsible manner that reflects credit on themselves and the college. The following misconduct on college facilities is subject to disciplinary action:

(13) Possession of firearms, licensed or unlicensed, except where possessed by commissioned police officers as prescribed by law.

Edmonds Community College

WAC 132Y-125-004 Disciplinary procedures. Enrollment in Edmonds Community College carries with it the obligation that the student will be a responsible citizen of the college. At the same time the college has the responsibility of informing students of their rights and responsibilities, defining reasonable standards of behavior, and assuring substantive and procedural due process.
The following procedures apply to the administration of disciplinary action for nonacademic violations.

(2) Guidelines for student conduct. The following are guidelines for acceptable student conduct. A student enrolling in the college assumes a responsibility for conduct compatible with the college's function as an educational institution. Although Edmonds Community College is dedicated to an open, free society, there are some actions incompatible with the mission of an institution of higher education. Grounds for disciplinary action shall include, but not be limited to, the following:

(m) Illegal possession or use of firearms, explosives, dangerous chemicals, substances or instruments or other weapons which can be used to inflict bodily harm on any individual or damage upon a building or grounds of the college or college-owned or controlled property or at college-sponsored or supervised functions.

Cascadia Community College

WAC 132Z-115-090 Code of conduct. Cascadia Community College expects that its students while within college facilities or attending a college-sponsored activity, will adhere to high standards of honor and good citizenship and that they will conduct themselves in a responsible manner that reflects credit on themselves and the college. The following misconduct is subject to disciplinary action:

(19) Possession of firearms, licensed or unlicensed, except where possessed by commissioned police officers as prescribed by law.

Shoreline Community College

WAC 132G-120-015 Grounds for discipline.

(2) Specific instances of misconduct for which the college will impose sanctions include, but are not limited to:

(h) Possession or use of unlawfully possessed firearms, explosives, dangerous chemicals or other dangerous weapons or instrumentalities on the college campus, except for authorized college purposes (legal defense sprays are exempt in this section).

Bellevue Community College

WAC 132H-120-200 Student responsibilities. Any student shall be subject to disciplinary action as provided for in this chapter, who either as a [principal] [principle] [actor or aide or abettor:] actor[,] aider, abettor or accomplice as defined in RCW 9A.08.020

(3) Commits any of the following acts which are hereby prohibited:
(k) Weapons. Possession or use of firearms, explosives, dangerous chemicals or other dangerous weapons or instrumentalities on the college campus, except for authorized college purposes or for law enforcement officers, unless written approval has been obtained from the dean of student services or any other person designated by the president.

Clark College

WAC 132N-150-240 Weapons on campus. Weapons, unless otherwise permitted by law, are not permitted on the college campus, at any other facilities leased or operated by the college, or at any activity under the administration or sponsorship of the college.

Exceptions to this policy are permitted when the weapon is used in conjunction with an approved college instructional program or is carried by a duly commissioned law enforcement officer or campus security officer.

Public Schools

WAC 72-140-080 Prohibited conduct at school facilities. (4) No person or group may use or enter onto school facilities having in their possession firearms or other weapons, even if licensed to do so, except duly appointed and commissioned law enforcement officers.

WAC 148-140-080 Prohibited conduct at school facilities. (4) No person or group may use or enter onto school facilities having in their possession firearms or other weapons, even if licensed to do so, except duly appointed and commissioned law enforcement officers.

Shelters For Victims of Domestic Violence

WAC 388-61A-0125 Where do I keep firearms and other dangerous weapons? (1) You must keep firearms and other dangerous weapons in a locked storage container, gun safe, or another storage area made of strong, unbreakable material.

(2) If the storage cabinet has a glass or another breakable front, you must secure the firearms with a locked cable or chain placed through the trigger guards.

(3) You must store ammunition in a place that is separate from the firearms or locked in a gun safe.

(4) You must allow access to firearms, weapons and ammunition only to authorized persons.

Day Care Centers

WAC 388-73-104 Firearms. (1) The licensee must not permit firearms, ammunition, and other weapons on the premises of child care agencies, except as allowed in family homes.

(2) In family homes, firearms, ammunition, and other weapons must be kept in secure, locked storage, at all times when not in use. They must be accessible only to authorized persons. Secure locked storage means a locked storage container, gun cabinet, gun safe, or other storage area made of strong, unbreakable material. If the cabinet has a glass or other breakable front, then the guns need to be secured with a cable or chain placed through the trigger guards securing the guns in the storage unit.

(3) The licensee must only allow firearm use under competent adult supervision and only if the youth has completed a gun safety or hunter safety course.

Race Tracks

WAC 260-20-075 Firearms prohibited on association grounds. Each racing association shall exclude from its grounds any person found to have firearms in his possession, except security personnel employed by the association or commission and law enforcement officers. Any licensee or permit holder who brings firearms onto the grounds of any racing association, except security personnel and law enforcement officers, may be subject to revocation or suspension of such license or permit, and any other authorized penalty the stewards may deem necessary.

Youth Shelters

WAC 388-160-210 Firearms and other weapons. An overnight youth shelter licensee shall ensure no firearms or other weapons are on the premises except those confiscated and secured from youth upon admission and these shall be locked up.

Milwaukee Road Corridor

WAC 332-52-067 Milwaukee Road Corridor — Restrictions on use. The following acts are prohibited on the corridor: (2) Public behavior

(d) Hunting or discharging of firearms, or having in possession shotguns or rifles. Other firearms will be unloaded and stored. No person shall discharge on any portion of the corridor a firearm, bow and arrow, or air or gas device or any device capable of injuring or killing any animal or person or damaging or destroying any public or private property. However, the department may allow hunting on portions of the corridor leased by or covered by an agreement with another public agency which owns or controls adjoining property.

Olympia Capitol Campus

WAC 236–12–470

(1) No person shall carry any firearm or other dangerous weapon as described in chapter 9.41 RCW on the state capitol grounds or in any building on the state capitol grounds: Provided, That this regulation shall not apply to duly authorized federal, state, and local law enforcement officers or to any federal, state, and local government employee authorized to carry firearms in the course of their public employment; and: Provided, That a person may carry a firearm in accordance with chapter 9.41 RCW.

(2) No person may carry into any building on the state capitol grounds any voice–amplification equipment, blow horns, sirens; or other similar noise–producing devices which may be used to disrupt the conduct of state business by state employees. [Statutory Authority: RCW 43.19.011, 43.19.125, and 46.08.150. 04–24–080, § 236–12–470, filed 12/1/04, effective 1/1/05. Statutory Authority: RCW 43.17.060, 43.19.125 and 46.08.150. 99–19–022, § 236–12–470, filed 9/7/99, effective 10/8/99; 81–11–001 (Order 81–1), § 236–12–470, filed 5/7/81; Order 76–7, § 236–12–470, filed 10/18/76.]

Use Of Force

RCW 9.01.055 (1969 c 37 § 1.) Citizen immunity if aiding officer, scope - When. Private citizens aiding a police officer, or other officers of the law in the performance of their duties as police officers or officers of the law, shall have the same civil and criminal immunity as such officer, as a result of any act or commission for aiding or attempting to aid a police officer or other officer of the law, when such officer is in imminent danger of loss of life or grave bodily injury or when such officer requests such assistance and when such action was taken under emergency conditions and in good faith.

RCW 9A.16.020 (1986 c 149 § 2; 1979 ex.s. c 244 §7; 1977 ex.s. c 80 § 13; 1975 1st ex.s. c 260 § 9A.16.020) Use of force - When lawful. The use, attempt or offer to use force upon or toward the person of another is not unlawful in the following cases:

(1) Whenever necessarily used by a public officer in the performance of a legal duty, or a person assisting the officer and acting under the officer's direction;

(2) Whenever necessarily used by a person arresting one who has committed a felony and delivering him or her to a public officer competent to receive him or her into custody;

(3) Whenever used by a party about to be injured, or by another lawfully aiding him or her, in preventing or attempting to prevent an offense against his or her person, or a malicious trespass, or other malicious interference with real or personal property lawfully in his or her possession, in case the force is not more than is necessary;

(4) Whenever reasonably used by a person to detain someone who enters or remains unlawfully in a building or on real property lawfully in the possession of such person, so long as such detention is reasonable in duration and manner to investigate the reason for the detained person's presence on the premises, and so long as the premises in question did not reasonably appear to be intended to be open to members of the public;

(5) Whenever used by a carrier of passengers or the carrier's authorized agent or servant, or other person assisting them at their request in expelling from a carriage, railway car, vessel, or other vehicle, a passenger who refuses to obey a lawful and reasonable regulation prescribed for the conduct of passengers, if such vehicle has first been stopped and the force used is not more than is necessary to expel the offender with reasonable regard to the offender's personal safety;

(6) Whenever used by any person to prevent a mentally ill, mentally incompetent, or mentally disabled person from committing an act dan-gerous to any person, or in enforcing necessary restraint for the protection or restoration to health of the person, during such period only as is necessary to obtain legal authority for the restraint or custody of the person.

RCW 9A.16.030 (1979 ex.s. c 244 § 8; 1975 1st ex.s. c 260 § 9A.16.030.) Homicide — When excusable. Homicide is excusable when committed by accident or misfortune in doing any lawful act by lawful means, without criminal negligence, or without any unlawful intent.

RCW 9A.16.040 (1986 c 209 § 2; 1975 1st ex.s. c 260 § 9A.16.040.) Justifiable homicide or use of deadly force by public officer, peace officer, person aiding.

(1) Homicide or the use of deadly force is justifiable in the following cases:

(a) When a public officer is acting in obedience to the judgment of a competent court; or

(b) When necessarily used by a peace officer to overcome actual resistance to the execution of the legal process, mandate, or order of a court or officer, or in the discharge of a legal duty.

(c) When necessarily used by a peace officer or person acting under the officer[1]s command and in the officer's aid:

(i) To arrest or apprehend a person who the officer reasonably believes has committed, has attempted to commit, is committing, or is attempting to commit a felony;

(ii) To prevent the escape of a person from a federal or state correctional facility or in retaking a person who escapes from such a facility; or

(iii) To prevent the escape of a person from a county or city jail or holding facility if the person has been arrested for, charged with, or convicted of a felony; or

(iv) To lawfully suppress a riot of the actor or another participant is armed with a deadly weapon.

(2) In considering whether to use deadly force under subsection (1)(c) of this section, to arrest or apprehend any person for the commission of any crime, the peace officer must have probable cause to believe that the suspect, if not apprehended, poses a threat of serious physical harm to the officer or a threat of serious physical harm to others. Among the circumstances which may be considered by peace officers as a "threat of serious physical harm" are the following:

(a) The suspect threatens a peace officer with a weapon or displays a weapon in a manner that could reasonably be construed as threatening; or

(b) There is probable cause to believe that the suspect has committed any crime involving the infliction or threatened infliction of serious physical harm.

Under these circumstances deadly force may also be used if necessary to prevent escape from the officer, where, if feasible, some warning is given.

(3) A public officer or peace officer shall not be held criminally liable for using deadly force without malice and with good faith belief that such act is justifiable pursuant to this section.

(4) This section shall not be construed as:

(a) Affecting the permissible use of force by a person acting under the authority of RCW 9A.16.020 or 9A.16.050; or

(b) Preventing a law enforcement agency from adopting standards pertaining to its use of deadly force that are more restrictive than this section.

Legislative Recognition: "The legislature recognizes that RCW 9A.16.040 establishes a dual standard with respect to the use of deadly force by peace officers and private citizens, and further recognizes that private citizens[1] permissible use of deadly force under the authority of RCW 9.01.200, 9A.16.020, or 9A.16.050 is not restricted and remains broader than the limitations imposed on peace officers." (1986 c 209 § 3.)

RCW 9A.16.050 (1975 1st ex.s. c 260 § 9A.16.050.) Homicide - By other person - When justifiable.

(1) In the lawful defense of the slayer, or his or her husband, wife, parent, child, brother, or sister, or any other person in his presence or company, when there is reasonable ground to apprehend a design on the part of the person slain to commit a felony or to do some great personal injury to the slayer or to any such person, and there is imminent danger of such design being accomplished; or

(2) In the actual resistance of an attempt to commit a felony upon the slayer, in his presence, or upon or in a dwelling, or other place of abode, in which he is.

RCW 9A.16.110 (1995 c 44 § 1; 1989 c 94 § 1; 1977 ex.s. c 206 § 8. Formerly RCW 9.01.200.) Defending against violent crime — Reimbursement.

(1) No person in the state shall be placed in legal jeopardy of any kind whatsoever for protecting by any reasonable means necessary, himself or herself, his or her family, or his or her real or personal property, or for coming to the aid of another who is in imminent danger of or the victim of assault, robbery, kidnapping, arson, burglary, rape, murder, or any other violent crime as defined in RCW 9.94A.030.

(2) When a person charged with a crime listed in subsection (1) of this section is found not guilty by reason of self-defense, the state of Washington shall reimburse the defendant for all reasonable costs, including loss of time, legal fees incurred, and other expenses involved in his or her defense. This reimbursement is not an independent cause of action. To award these reasonable costs the trier of fact must find that the defendant's claim of self-defense was sustained by a preponderance of the evidence. If the trier of fact makes a determination of self-defense, the judge shall determine the amount of the award.

(3) Notwithstanding a finding that a defendant's actions were justified by self-defense, if the trier of fact also determines that the defendant was engaged in criminal conduct substantially related to the events giving rise to the charges filed against the defendant the judge may deny or reduce the amount of the award. In determining the amount of the award, the judge shall also consider the seriousness of the initial criminal conduct. Nothing in this section precludes the legislature from using the sundry claims process to grant an award where none was granted under this section or to grant a higher award than one granted under this section.

(4) Whenever the issue of self-defense under this section is decided by a judge, the judge shall consider the same questions as must be answered in the special verdict under subsection (4) [(5)] of this section.

(5) Whenever the issue of self-defense under this section has been submitted to a jury, and the jury has found the defendant not guilty, the court shall instruct the jury to return a special verdict in substantially the following form:

Answer "Yes" or "No":

1. Was the finding of not guilty based upon self-defense? ______
2. If your answer to question 1 is no, do not answer the remaining questions.
3. If your answer to question 1 is yes, was the defendant:
   a. Protecting himself or herself? ______
   b. Protecting his or her family? ______
   c. Protecting his or her property? ______
   d. Coming to the aid of another who was in imminent danger of a heinous crime? ______
   e. Coming to the aid of another who was the victim of a heinous crime?

______

f. Engaged in criminal conduct substantially related to the events giving rise to the crime with which the defendant is charged? ______

NOTES:

Use of deadly force — Legislative recognition: See note following RCW 9A.16.040.

Child Proofing Your Guns

Tragedies in Springfield, Ore., Littleton, Colo., Moses Lake, Wash. and elsewhere have resulted in increased attention toward kids and guns. If you have children, it is your responsibility to teach them about gun safety and respect at an early age.

Here's what not to do:

Don't buy a handgun for personal protection, take it home, load it, then hide it in the bureau drawer. The child in your home is guaranteed by nature to find it, and wait until you aren't looking to play with it.

Don't take the gun home, show it to the child, then admonish the youngster to NEVER touch it!

Don't violate state and federal laws by purchasing handguns for your underage child, especially if that youngster has exhibited any type of repetitive discipline or anger management problem.

Here's what you should do:

Explain to the youngster who is old enough to understand that this is **your** gun. *It is not a toy.*

Assure the youngster that if he or she is curious about the firearm, you need only be asked, and you will be happy to show it to the youngster and explain how it works. And keep your word about this. A child who is promised something, then disappointed, is not going to believe your promise the next time. That child is going to decide to check the gun out on his/her own. After making sure the gun is not loaded, let the curious child handle it, and feel its weight.

At your first opportunity, take the child with you to the shooting range. Fit the youngster with good eye and hearing protection, let him or her see you doing the same, then fire a few shots.

Afterward, invite the youngster to help you clean the gun. This is where the kid typically gets turned off. It worked at my house.

When storing the firearm, store it UNLOADED and keep the ammunition separate. Many people select trigger locks, gun safes or other security devices as added protection. That's your choice.

As a responsible gun owner, it is incumbent upon you to take whatever steps are necessary to keep guns out of the wrong hands, especially young hands. We all suffer when tragedy strikes.

Pay attention to your kids. Tell them you love them. And mean it.

Holding Suspects at Gunpoint

With the State Supreme Court's affirmation of "no duty to retreat," private citizens may legally stand their ground, but don't be foolish. Avoid trouble when possible.

If you are in a confrontation that has deteriorated to the point that you are holding someone at gunpoint, you must maintain control of the situation by all means available.

Realistically, if you are in a confrontation that has deteriorated to the point that you are holding someone at gunpoint, you better mean business and you should telegraph that to your adversary by all means available, both verbal and by your actions.

• Use "command language." Let the suspect know you are in control.

• Initially, if you are facing the suspect, keep your muzzle trained at an area below the belt line, finger off the trigger. Yes, this flies in the face of the "center of mass" philosophy, but remember, you're holding the suspect until police arrive, you're not actually shooting him.

With the gun aimed low, you can still see clearly if he attempts to move his arms or hands toward a concealed weapon. In the event you have to suddenly shoot, the bullet angle is downward. A bullet passing through a suspect at that angle is less likely to be a danger to innocent bystanders.

• Order the suspect to the ground SLOWLY, one leg then one hand at a time, so you can keep his hands in sight. You may not want to yell at someone repeatedly to "Get On The Ground!" like they do on COPS. Get him down on his stomach, arms and legs spread out, palms turned upward. Have him turn his face away from you, so you can cover him without him seeing you. At this point, you may want to holster your gun (hand on the grip) or lower it to your side, in anticipation of the police arriving. Don't take your eyes off him.

• Expect the suspect to first yell at you, typically with obscenities. He may threaten you if you do not allow him to escape. As it becomes evident the police are coming and that your resolve is not shaken by his threats, anticipate his tone to change as he starts pleading with you to let him go.

• If he attempts to get up and move toward you, despite your instructions to stay put, you can reasonably conclude he will attempt to disarm you and injure or kill you.

• Have someone greet the police at the door, and position yourself in a way that you will be facing them and still watching the suspect. This person is your "welcoming committee." If the police order you to drop your gun, do it, safely as possible, ideally so it lands on its side, and out of reach of the suspect, and where you can put your foot on it.

You will get additional expert advice on this subject by attending a good shooting school. Some instructors may offer different suggestions.

Don't debate techniques . . . Learn something new!

NOTES